NOTE-FOR-NOTE KEYBOARD TRANSCRIPTIONS

ROCK KEYBOARD/ORGAN HITS

MW00988877

ISBN 978-1-4950-1226-6

HAL•LEONARD®
CORPORATION
7777 W. BLUEMOUND RD. P.O. BOX 13819 MILWAUKEE, WI 53213

Visit Hal Leonard Online at
www.halleonard.com

Abacab

Words and Music by Tony Banks, Phil Collins and Mike Rutherford

and stare. ____ (Ab - a - cab) is - n't an - y - where.

(Ab - a- cab.)

Synth
Analog lead

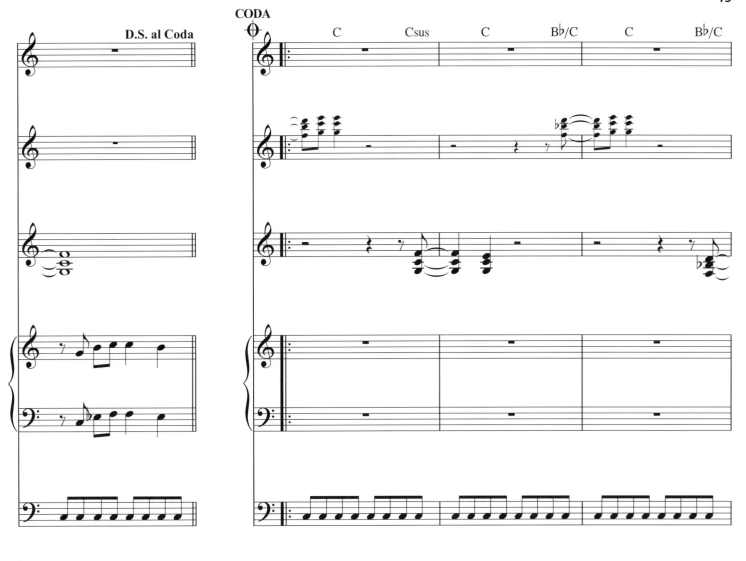

Born to Be Wild

Words and Music by Mars Bonfire

take the world in a love em - brace, ___ fire all of your guns ___

Play fill 1 (2nd time)
Play fill 2 (3rd time)

___ at once, ___ and let's float in - to space. _____

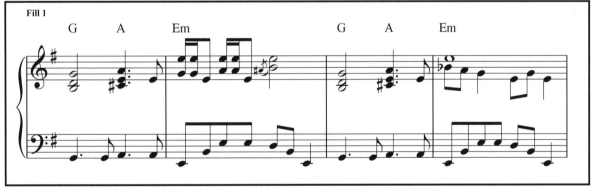

Fill 1

Fill 2

To Coda ⊕

Born to be wild.

California Sun

Words and Music by Morris Levy and Henry Glover

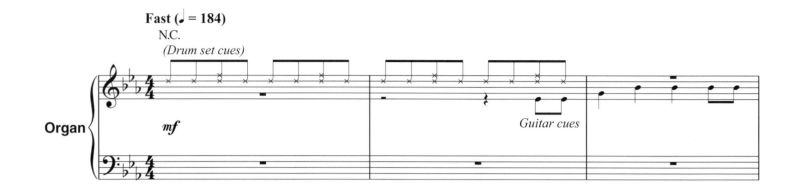

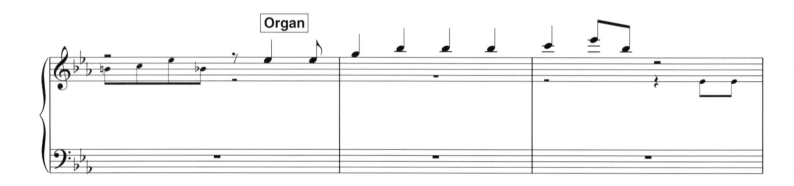

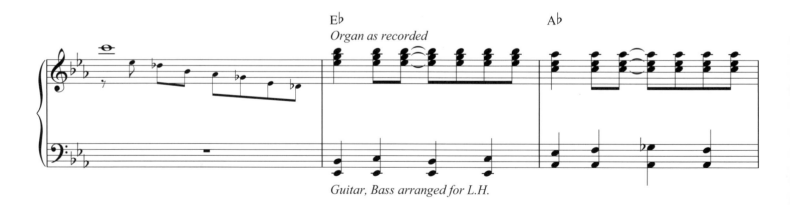

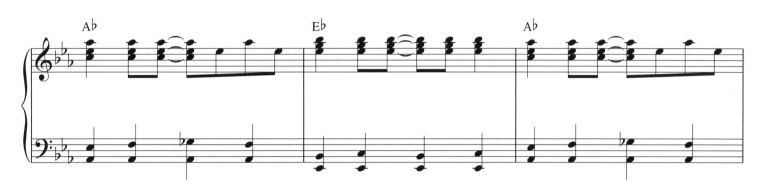

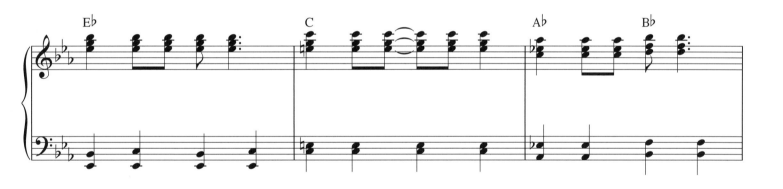

Well,— I'm go - ing out west where I be - long,
go - ing out west, out on the coast,
girls — are frisk - y in old 'Fris - co,

Guitar cues

and I'll ___ fly. Well, they're out there a - hav - ing fun ___

in that warm Cal - i - for - nia sun. ___ Well, ___ I'm

warm Cal - i - for - nia sun. ___

Dirty Work

Words and Music by Walter Becker and Donald Fagen

find your-self some-bod-y who can do _____ the job ____ for free. ____ When you
sent the maid home ear-ly, like, a thou - sand times _ be - fore. ____ Like the

need a bit of lov - ing 'cause your man ___ is out of town, _ that's the
cas - tle in his cor - ner in a me - di - e - val game, _ I fore -

time to get me run-ning, and you know ____ I'll be a - round. ___ }
see ter - ri - ble trou - ble, and I stay ____ here just the same. ___ }

I'm a fool ___ to do ___ your _ dirt - y work, oh ___ yeah. _____

Organ
Play 2nd time only

I don't wan - na do ___ your ___ dirt - y work no ___ more. _____

I'm a fool ___ to do ___ your ___ dirt - y work, oh ___ yeah. _____

Saxophone solo (cues)

(Solo ends)

I'm a fool_ to do_ your_ dirt-y work, oh_ yeah.___

I don't wan - na do__ your_ dirt - y work no__ more.___

Do You Feel Like We Do

Words and Music by Peter Frampton, John Siomos, Rick Wills and Mick Gallagher

Woke up this morn - ing with a wine glass in my hand.

Comp ad lib.

Whose __ wine? What __ wine? Where the hell did I dine? _____

(continue simile)

Must have been a dream; _ I don't be - lieve where I've been. _____

Come on, _ I'm gon-na do it a - gain. _____

Do you, ___ you ___   feel like I do? ___

42

do?_____

Guitar solo ad lib.

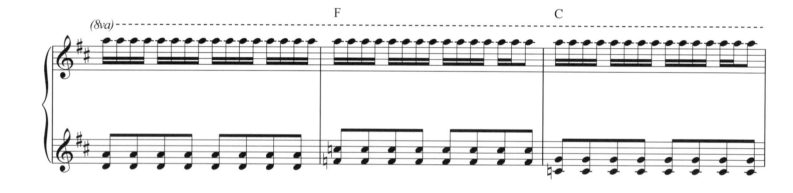

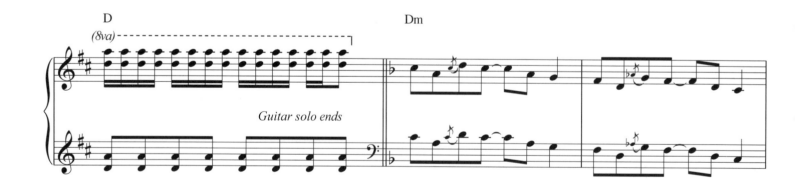

Guitar solo ends

rit.

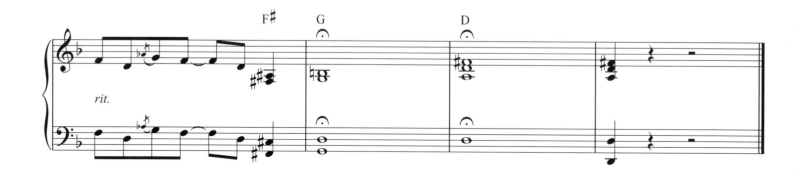

Fly Like an Eagle

Words and Music by Steve Miller

Synth 2: White noise is filtered/modulated throughout, to produce different resonant and pulsing effects.

**Synth 1: *Analog synth effects with heavy delay/reverb; written rhythms are approximate representations of recorded part.*

Tick, tock, _ tick. Dut-dut-du-du.

Tick, tock, _ tick. Dut-dut - du-du.

Tick, tock, _ tick. Dut - dut - du-du.

Time keeps on slip - pin', slip - pin', slip - pin' in - to the fu -

- ture. _____

Synth 1

Time keeps on slip-pin', slip-pin', slip-pin' in - to the fu - ture. _____

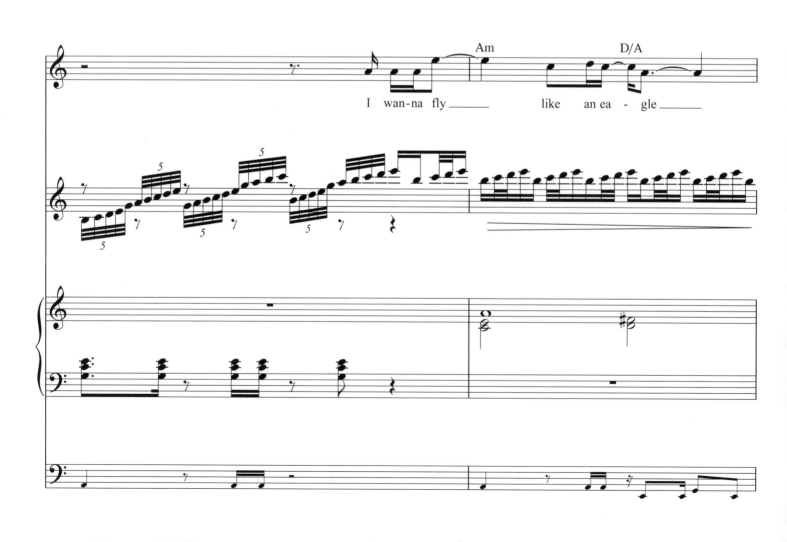

I wan-na fly _____ like an ea - gle _____

lu - tion. _____ Feed the ba - bies who

don't have e - nough _ to eat, shoe the child - ren with no

shoes on _ their feet, house the peo - ple liv - ing in _ the street.

Time keeps on slip-pin', slip-pin', slip-pin' in-to the fu - ture. _____

Du - dut - n-du-dut.   Du - dut - n-du-dut.

Du - dut - n-du-dut.   Du - dut - n - du - dut.   Du-dut-n-du-dut.

-ture. _____

Time   keeps on slip - pin', slip - pin',

Synth 1

slip-pin'   in - to   the   fu - ture.

Freely

rit.

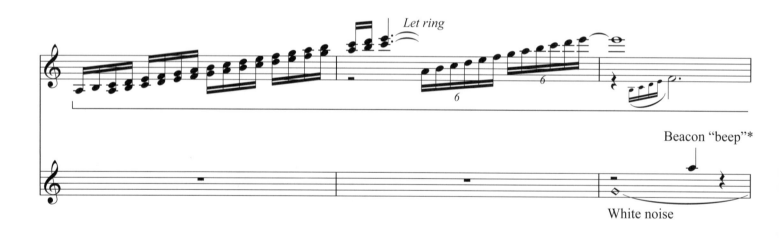

Let ring

Beacon "beep"*

White noise

Repeat and fade out

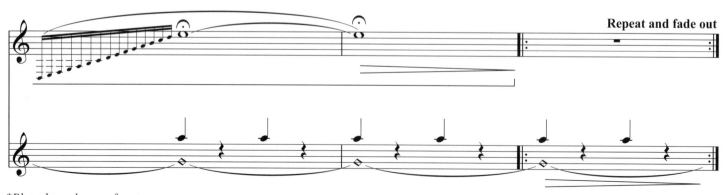

*Played evenly over free tempo.

Fooling Yourself
(The Angry Young Man)

Words and Music by Tommy Shaw

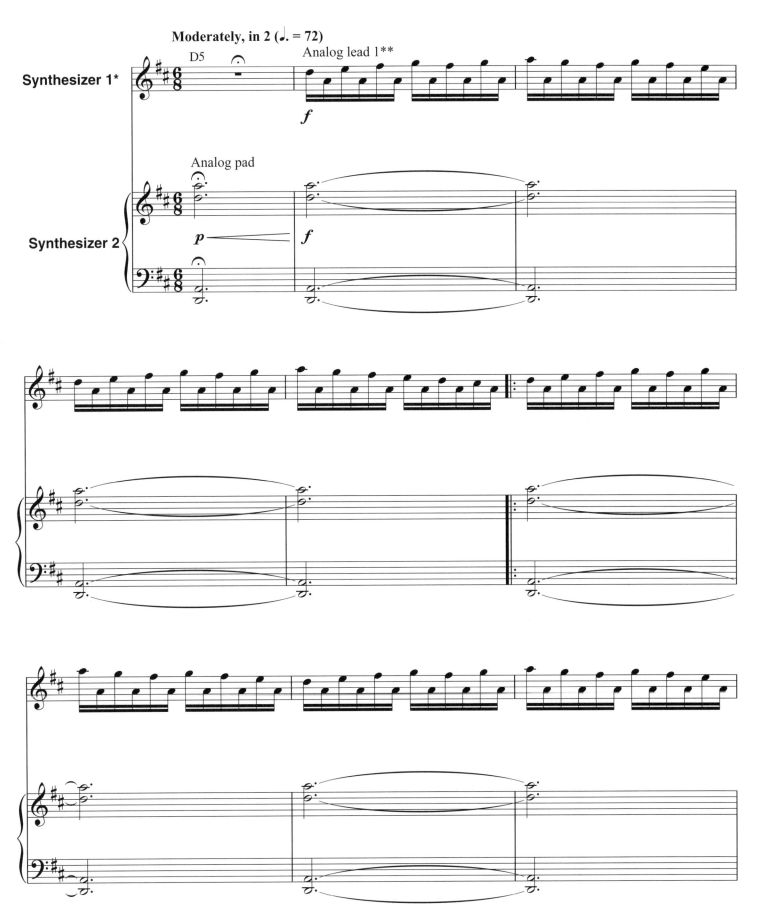

*All Synthesizer 1 lead patches use slight portamento
**Analog lead 1 sounds in multiple octaves. The most prominent sounding pitch is written.

*Analog lead 1, modified to sound in one octave only.

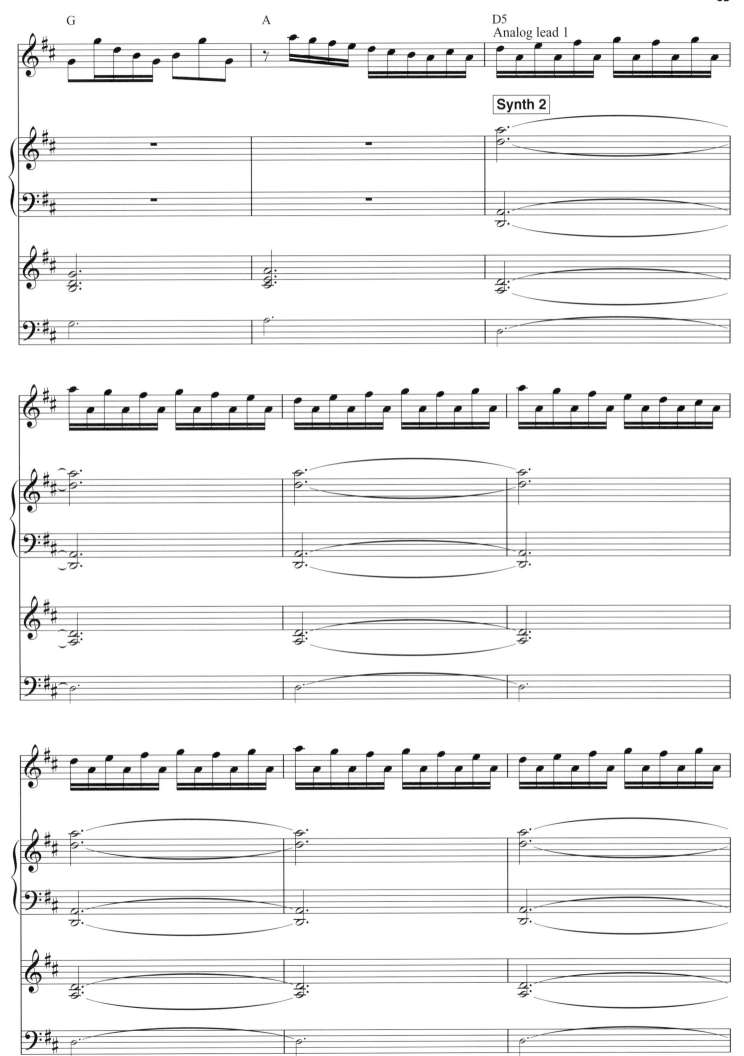

72

Gimme Some Lovin'

Words and Music by Steve Winwood, Muff Winwood and Spencer Davis

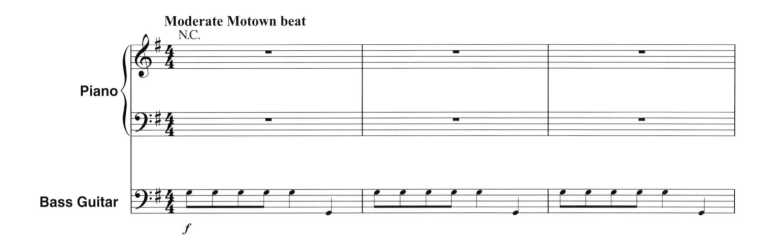

Bass continues

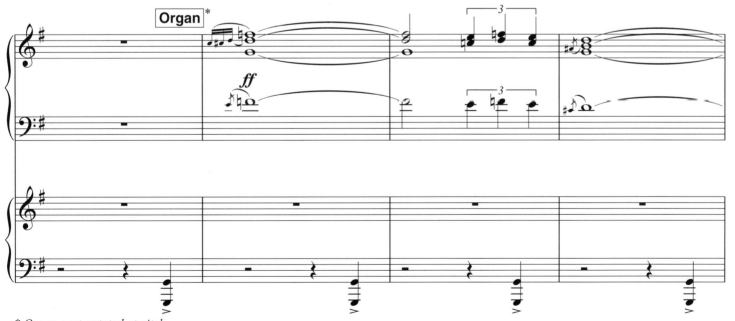

* Organ part notated at pitch.

want-ing some more. __ Oh, let me in, ba - by. I don't know what you've got, __ but you

bet - ter take it eas - y, 'cause this place is hot. And I'm

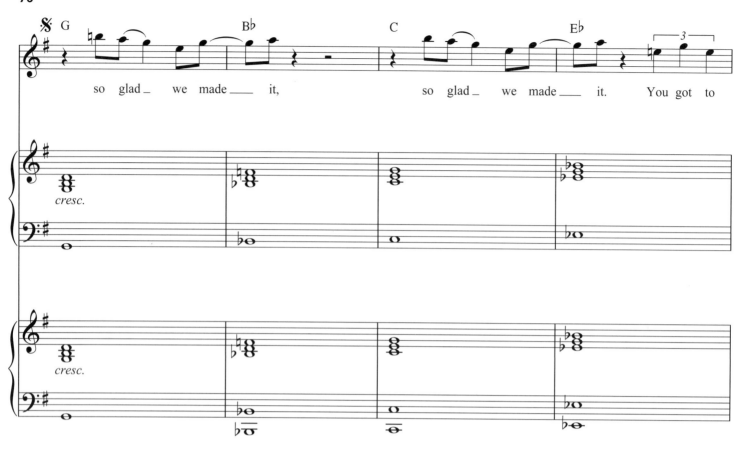

so glad __ we made __ it, so glad __ we made __ it. You got to

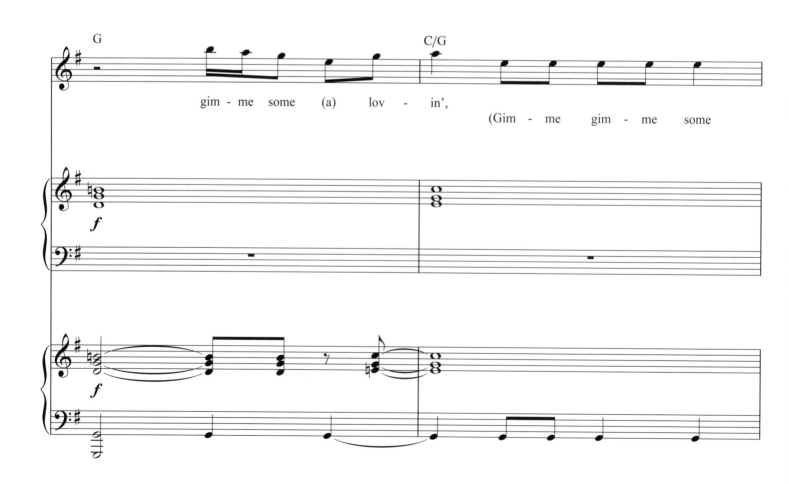

gim - me some (a) lov - in', (Gim - me gim - me some

gim-me some (a) lov - in',
lov - in',
gim - me gim - me some lov - in',
gim-me some (a) lov -

C/G
N.C.
Omit 2nd Time

in', ev -'ry day. __
ev -'ry day.) __

Bass

Bass continues

78

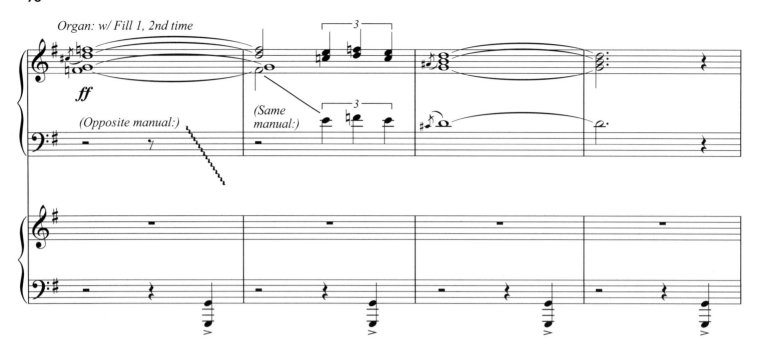

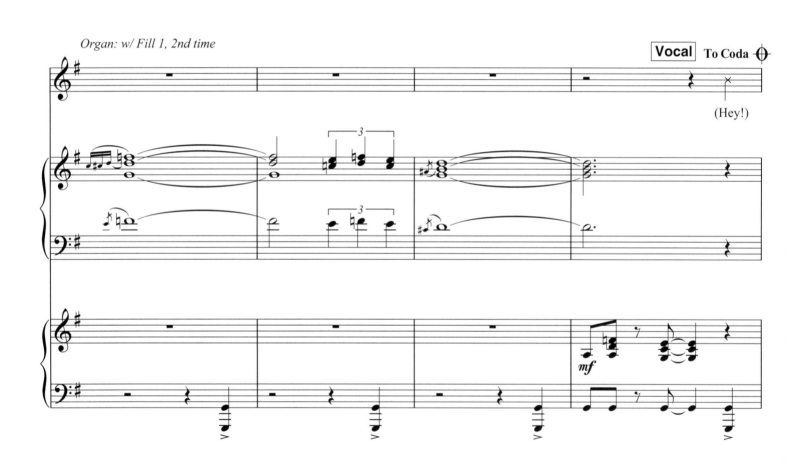

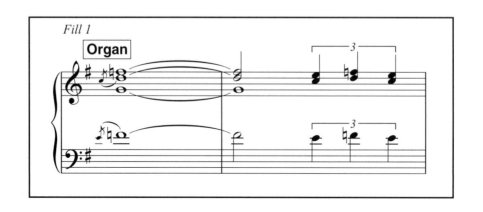

Well, I feel ___ so good, ___ ev - 'ry -

thing is sound-ing hot. ___ You bet - ter take it eas - y, 'cause the place is on fire. ___

Been a hard day, __ and I don't know what to do. __ We made it ba - by, and it

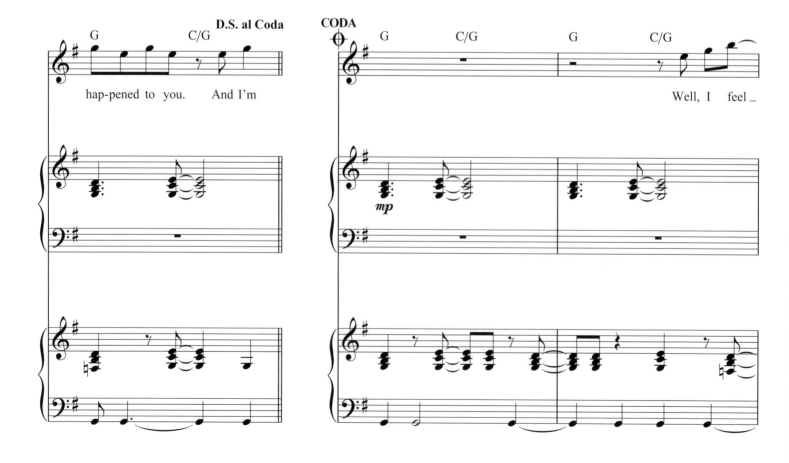

D.S. al Coda

hap-pened to you. And I'm

CODA

Well, I feel __

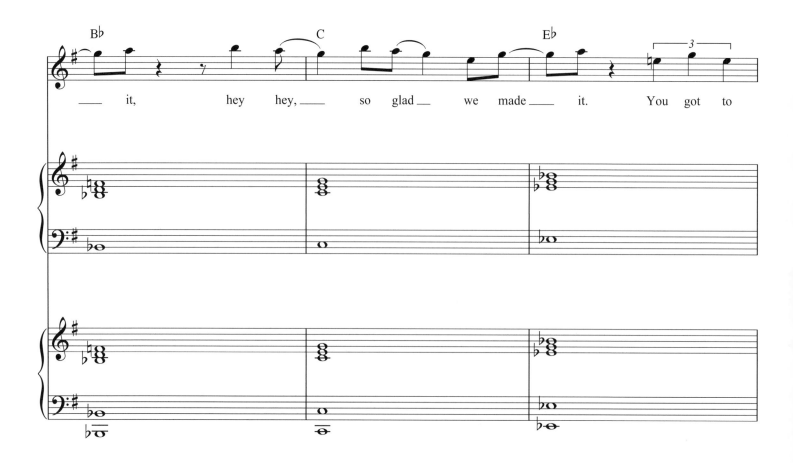

gim-me some (a) lov - in',   gim-me some (a) lov -
(Gim - me gim - me some   lov - in',

in',   woo ___   hoo! _____ *Vocal continues ad lib....*
gim - me gim - me some   lov - in',...)

Green Onions

Written by Al Jackson, Jr., Lewis Steinberg,
Booker T. Jones and Steve Cropper

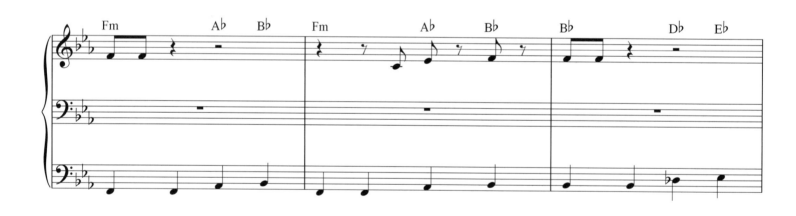

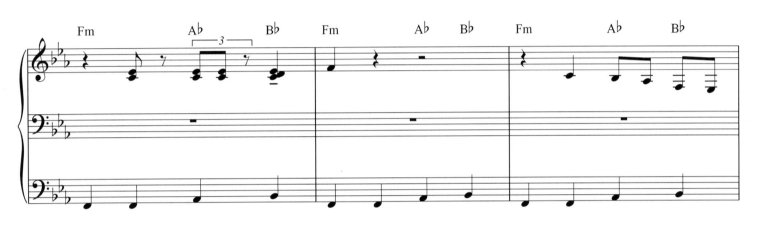
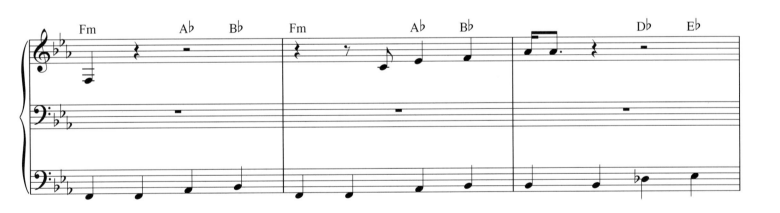
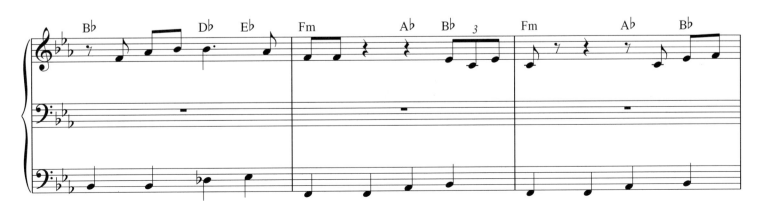

88

Guitar arranged for keyboard.

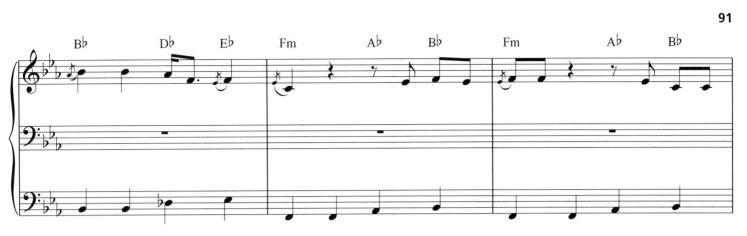

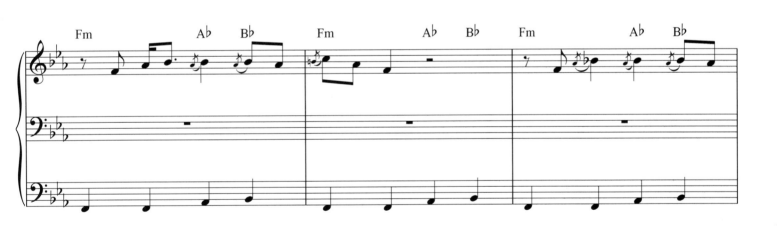

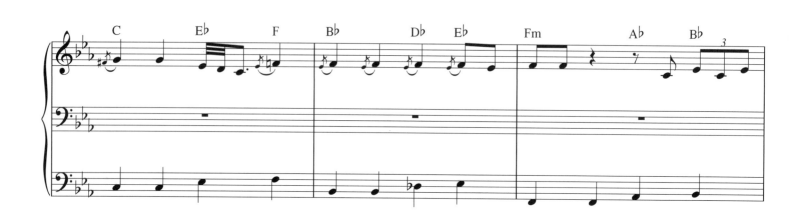

Guitar solo ad lib.

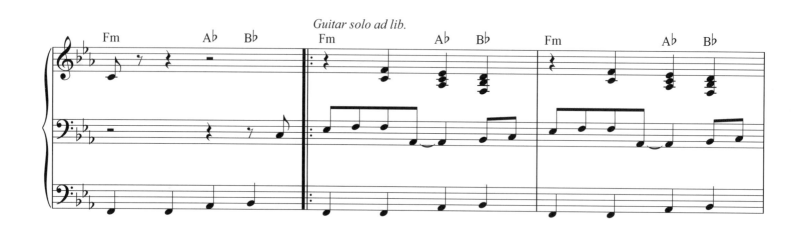

Repeat and Fade | **Optional Ending**

Highway Star

Words and Music by Ritchie Blackmore, Ian Gillan,
Roger Glover, Jon Lord and Ian Paice

Distorted Organ

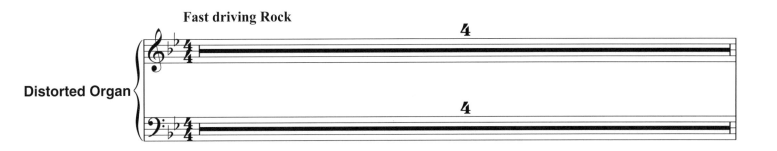

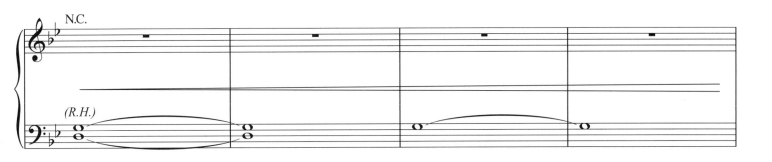

I bleed ___ it.
I seen ___ her.
I seen ___ it.

Yeah, ___ it's a wild ___
Yeah, ___ she turns ___
Eight cyl - in - ders, all ___

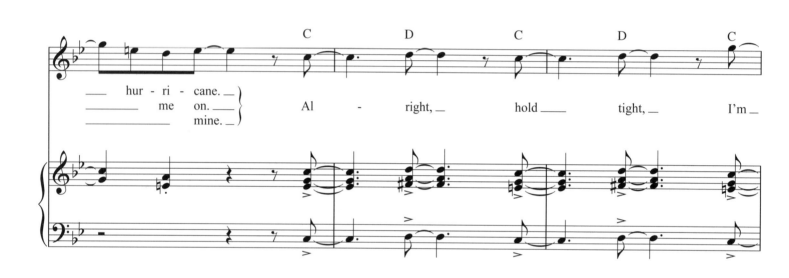

___ hur - ri - cane. ___
___ me on. ___
___ mine. ___

Al - right, ___ hold ___ tight, ___ I'm ___

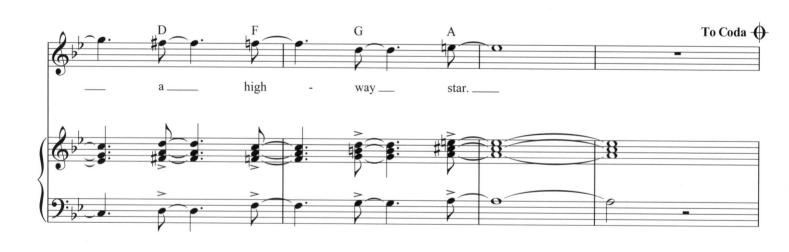

___ a ___ high - way ___ star. ___

To Coda

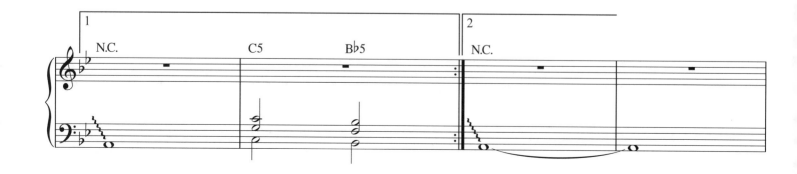

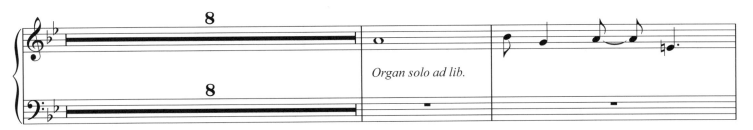

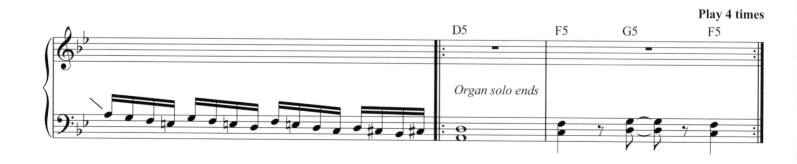

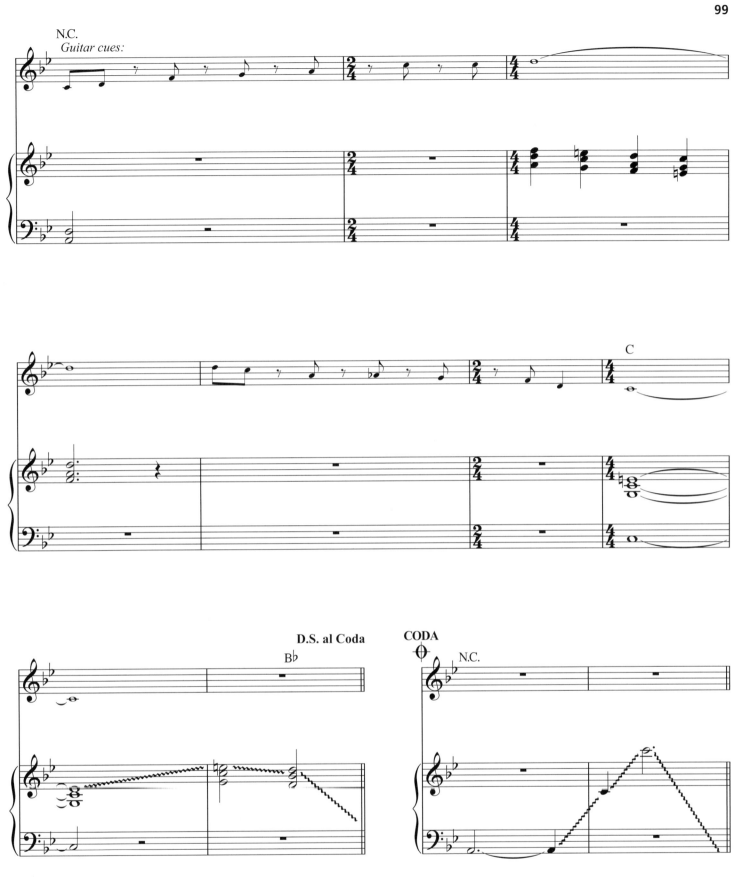

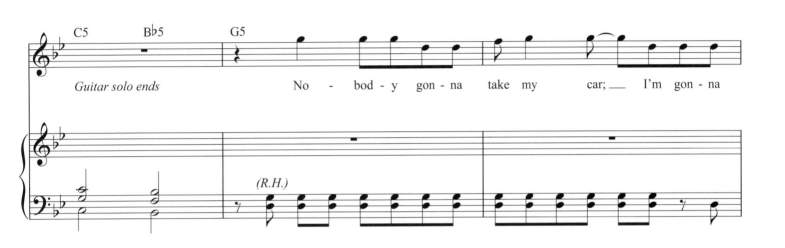

Guitar solo ends

No - bod - y gon - na take my car; — I'm gon - na

(R.H.)

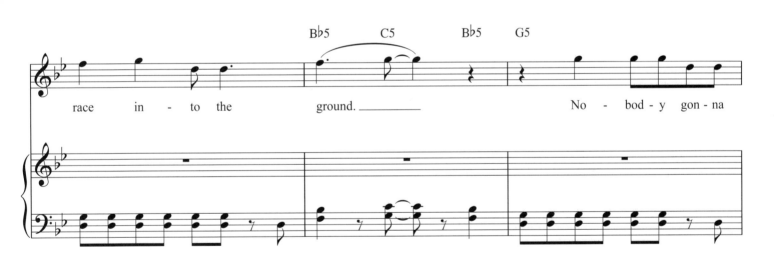

race in - to the ground. _____ No - bod - y gon - na

beat my car; — it's gon - na break the speed of sound. _____

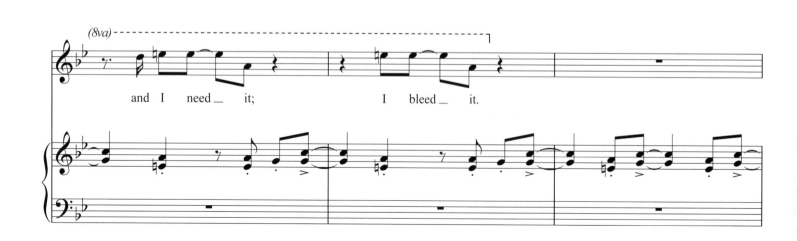

Hold Your Head Up

Words and Music by Rod Argent and Chris White

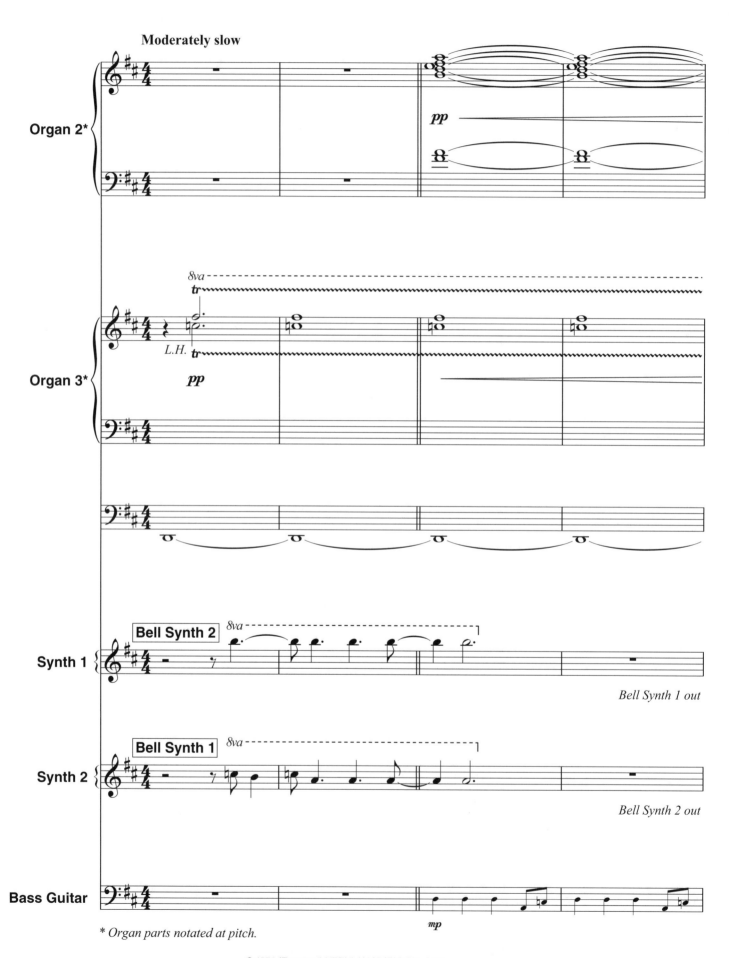

Organ parts notated at pitch.

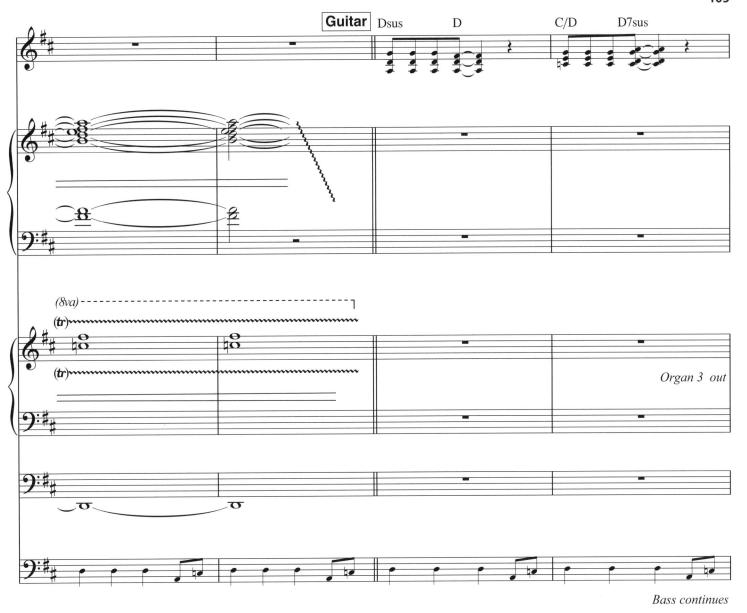

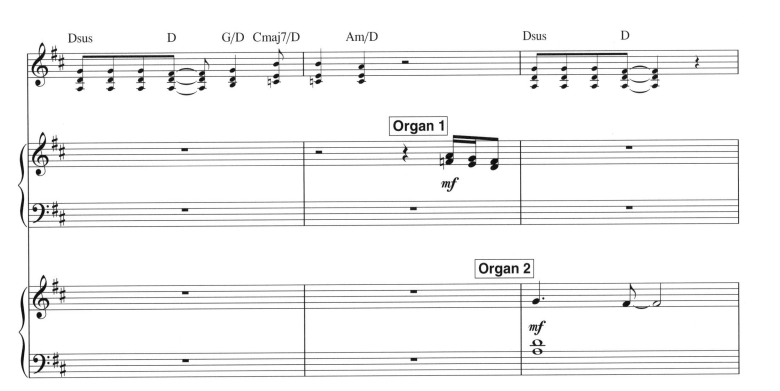

And if it's bad, _____ don't let it get you down; _ you can take_
And if they stare, _____ just let them burn their eyes _ on you mov -

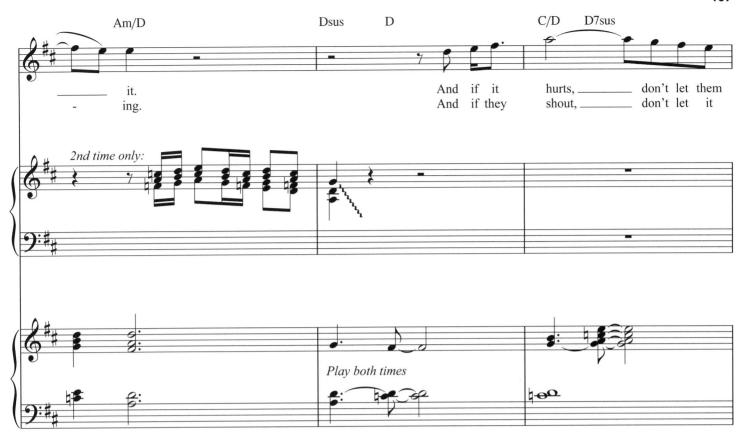

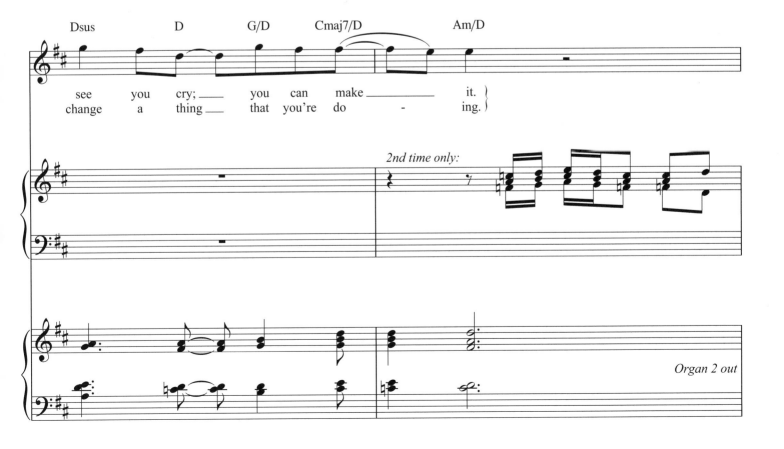

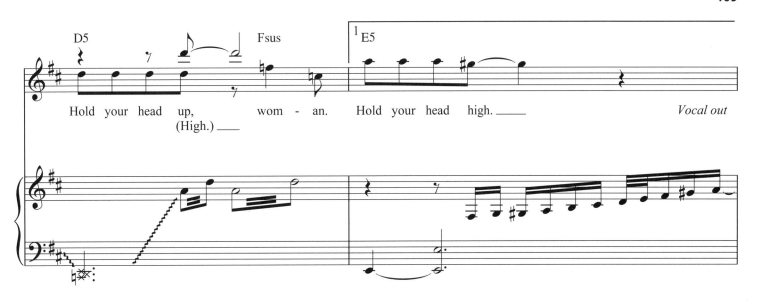

Hold your head up, wom - an. Hold your head high. _____ *Vocal out*
(High.) _____

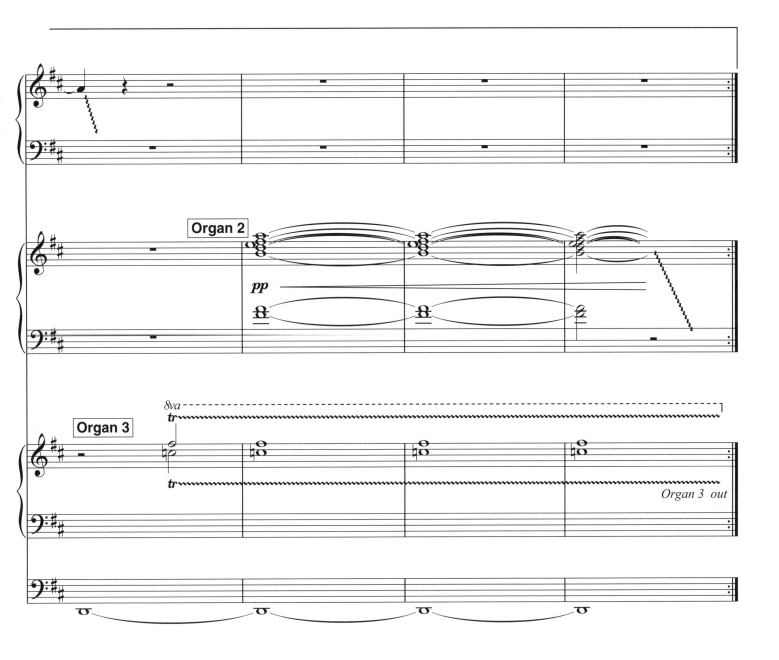

Hold your head high. ____

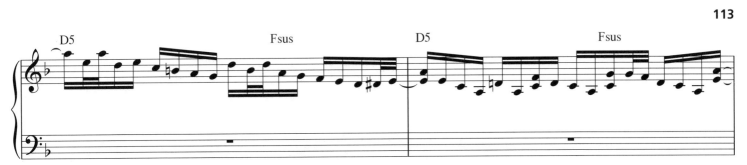

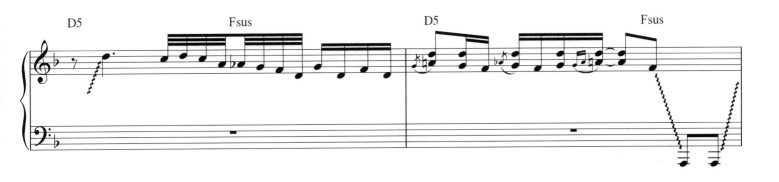

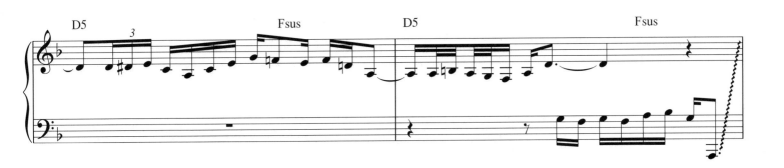

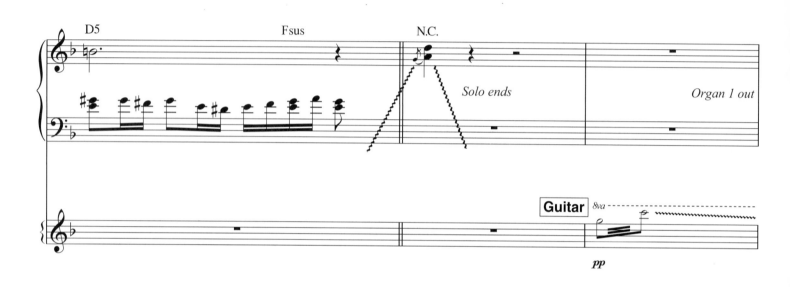

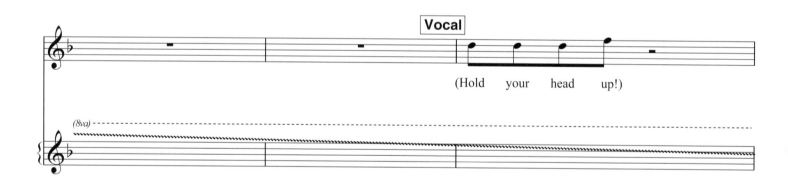

(Hold your head up!)

(Hold your head up!)   (Hold your head up!)   (Hold your head up!)

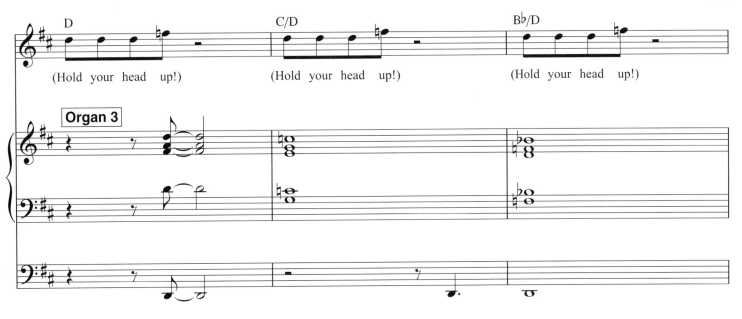

(Hold your head up!) (Hold your head up!) (Hold your head up!)

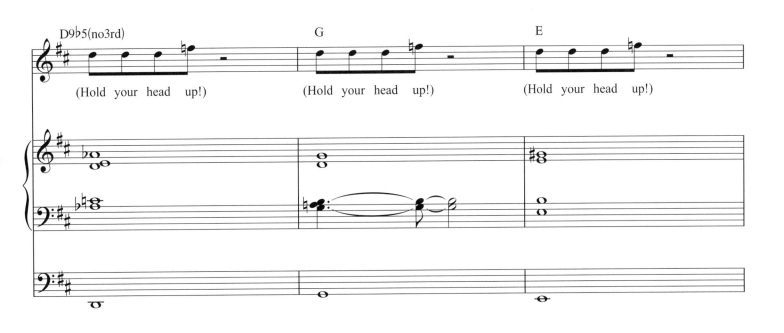

(Hold your head up!) (Hold your head up!) (Hold your head up!)

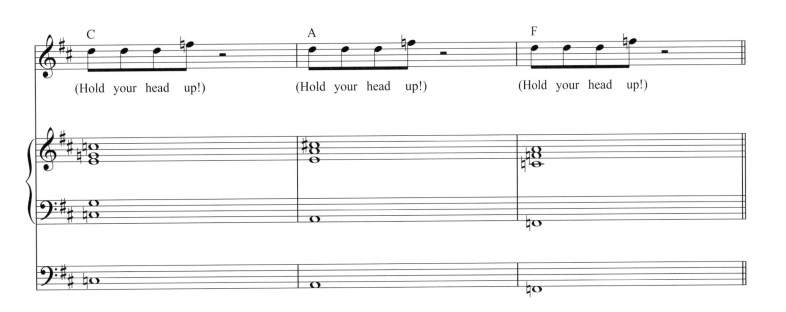

(Hold your head up!) (Hold your head up!) (Hold your head up!)

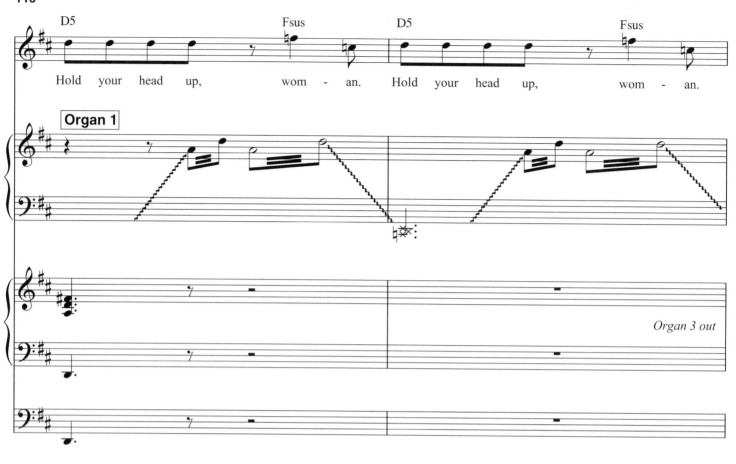

Organic 1

Hold your head up, wom-an. Hold your head up, wom-an.

Organ 3 out

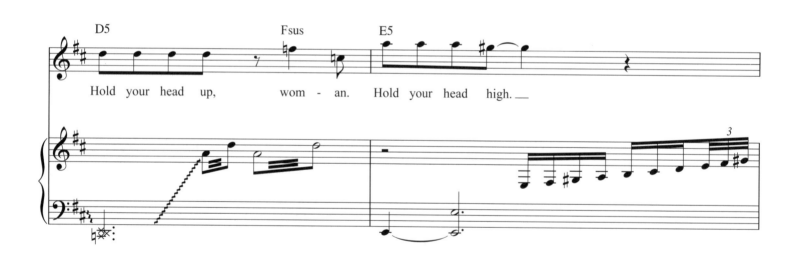

Hold your head up, wom-an. Hold your head high. __

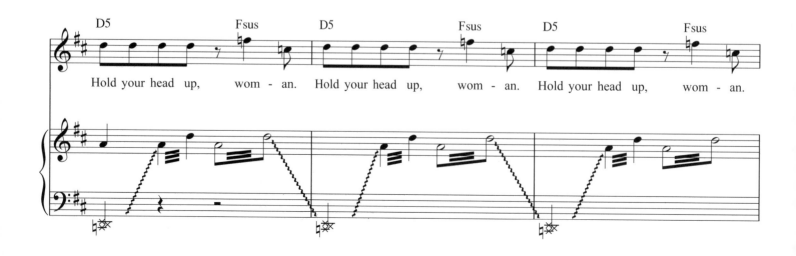

Hold your head up, wom-an. Hold your head up, wom-an. Hold your head up, wom-an.

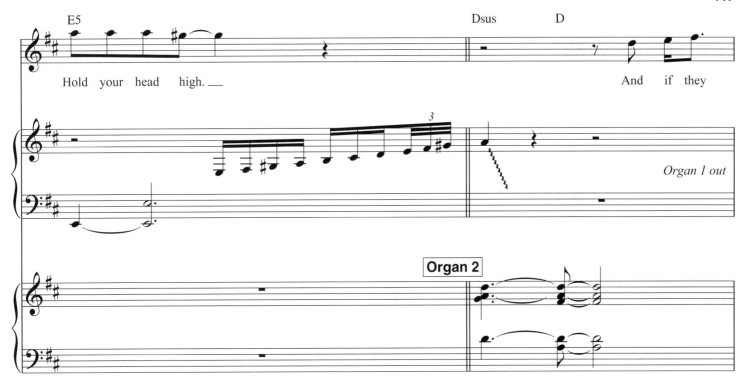

Hold your head high. ___ And if they

Organ 1 out

Organ 2

stare, ___ just let them burn their eyes ___ on you mov - ing.

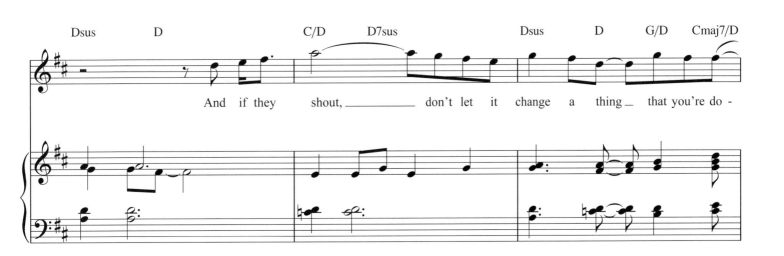

And if they shout, ___ don't let it change a thing ___ that you're do -

Hold your head up.

The House of the Rising Sun

Words and Music by Alan Price

123

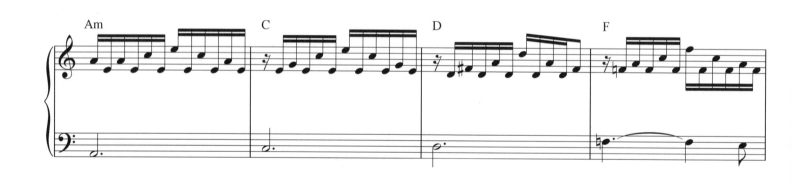

Oh!

I'm a Believer

Words and Music by Neil Diamond

132

In-A-Gadda-Da-Vida

Words and Music by Doug Ingle

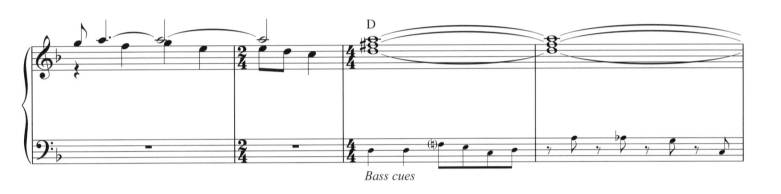

and take my hand? Oh, won't you

come with me and walk this land?

Please take my hand.

Spoken: Let me tell you now.

R.H.: Upper Manual
L.H.: Lower Manual

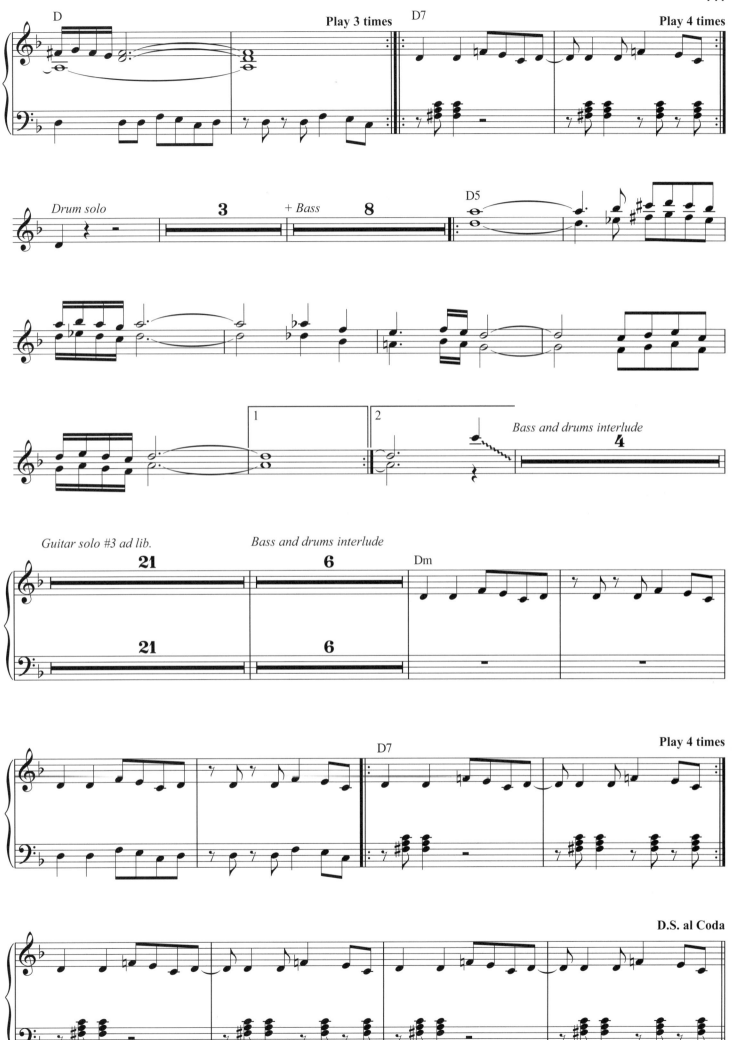

CODA

D5   N.C.

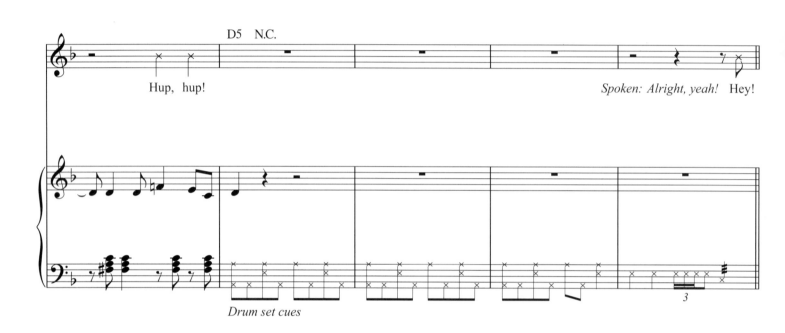

Hup, hup!

Spoken: Alright, yeah!   Hey!

Drum set cues

3

Dm

1 - 3

4

Rhythm section cues

Like a Rolling Stone

Words and Music by Bob Dylan

144

148

like a com-plete un - known, _____ like a roll - ing stone? _____

Ah, _____ prin-cess _ on the stee-ple, and all _ the

pret - ty peo - ple, they're all ___ drink - ing, think-ing that they've _ got it made, _

with no ___ di - rec - tion home, ___

like a com - plete un - known, ___

like a roll - ing stone? _

Optional Ending

The Logical Song

Words and Music by Rick Davies and Roger Hodgson

158

spect - a - ble, oh, pre - sent - a - ble, a veg - 'ta - ble." Oh, _____

_____ take, take, take it, yeah.

Sax solo as recorded

To Synth (Strings)

Well, at night, ___ when all ___

164

Ooh, and it's get-ting un-be-

liev - a - ble.

Repeat ad lib. and Fade

Optional Ending

Love the One You're With

Words and Music by Stephen Stills

you had. ___ There's a girl ___ right next to you ___

___ and ___ she's just wait - ing for some - thing to

do. ___ And there's a rose ___ in a fist - ed

Organ 2

Downstems: Bass cues.

glove, ___ and the ea - gle flies with the dove; ___

Many Rivers to Cross

Words and Music by Jimmy Cliff

96 Tears

Words and Music by Rudy Martinez

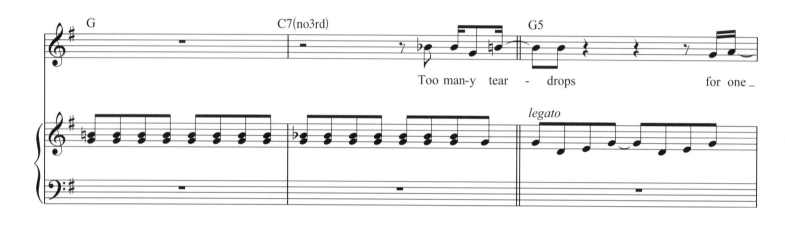

Too man-y tear - drops for one __

__ heart to be cry - ing; too man-y tear-

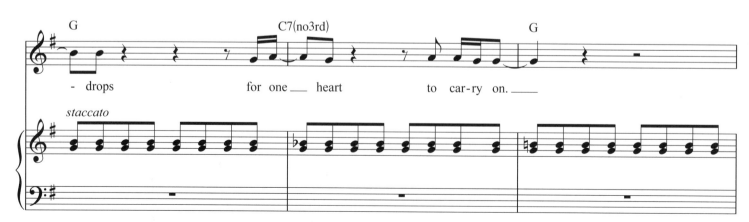

- drops for one __ heart to car-ry on. __

* *Organ parts notated at pitch.*

You're way on top, now, since you left

me. You're al - ways laugh - ing

way down at me. ___ But watch out now; ___

I'm gon - na get there. ___

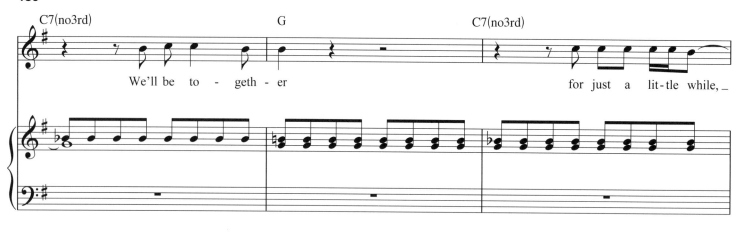

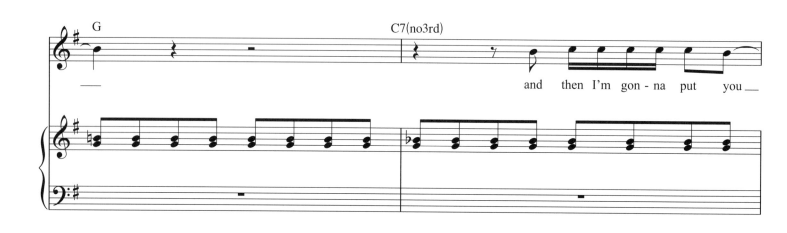

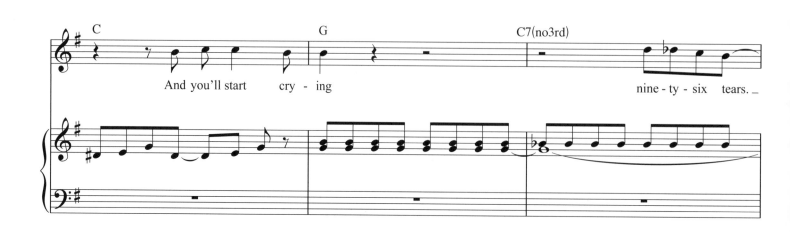

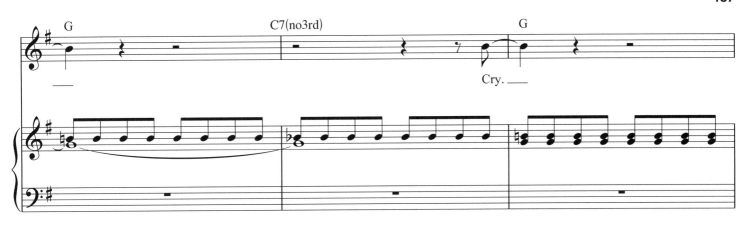

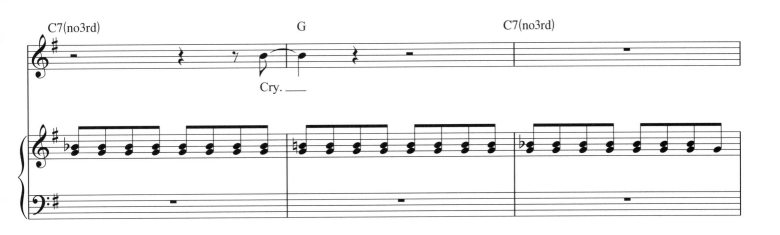

And when the sun comes up, ___ I'll be on top. ___

You'll be right down there, _ look-ing up. And I might wave,

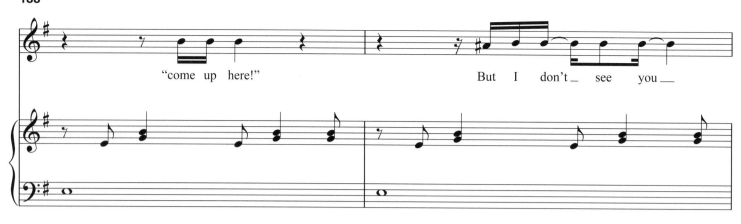

"come up here!" But I don't ___ see you ___

wav - ing now. I'm way ___ down here, ___

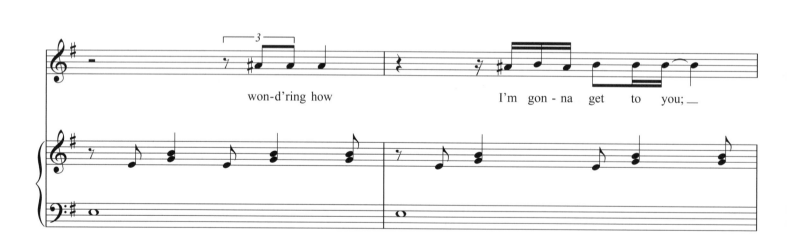

won-d'ring how I'm gon - na get to you; ___

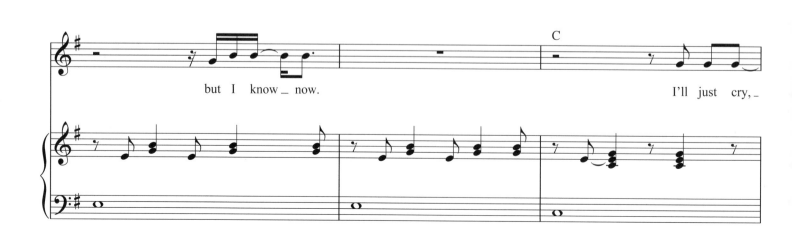

but I know ___ now. I'll just cry, ___

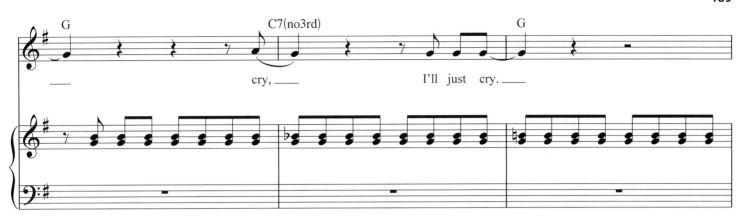
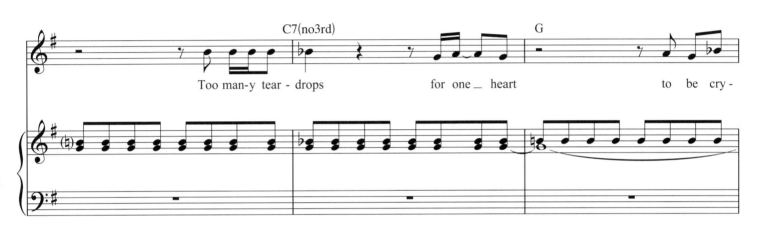
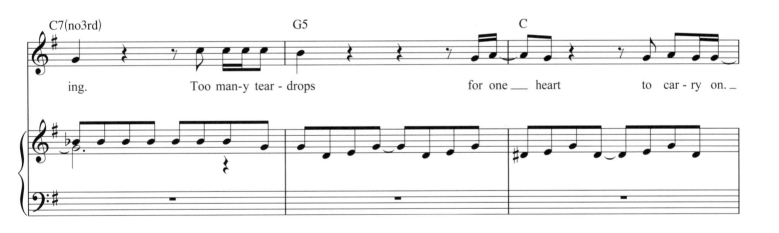

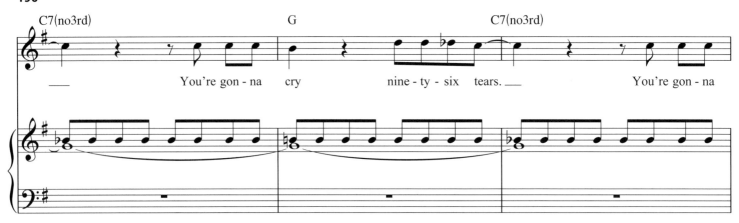

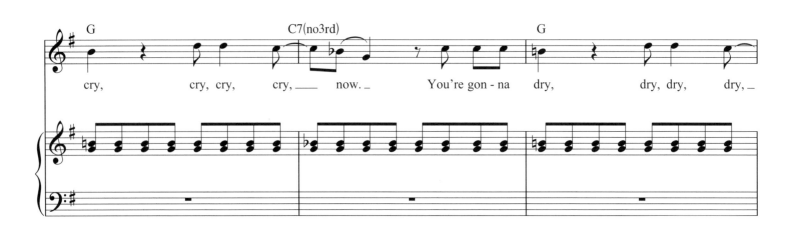

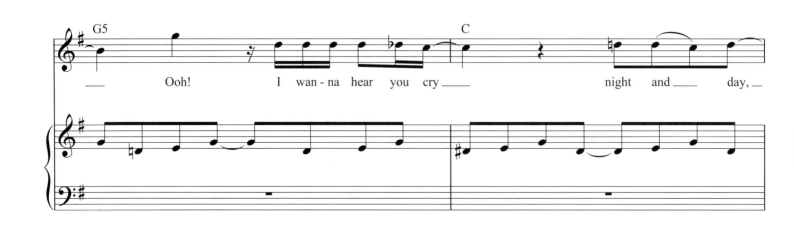

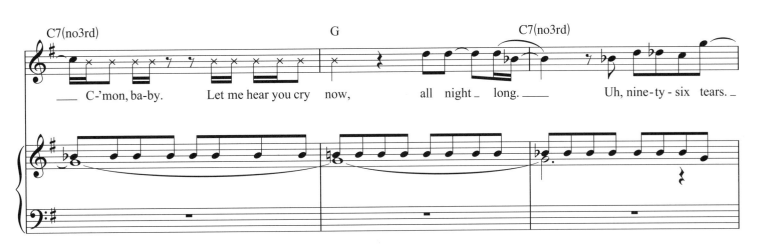

Refugee

Words and Music by Tom Petty and Mike Campbell

Guitar solo ad lib.

Some-where, some - how, some - bod - y must have kicked you a - round _____ some.

Who knows, _ may-be you were kid - napped, tied _____ up, tak - en a - way _ and held _ for ran -

(don't have to live like a ref - u - gee). _____ Girl, you don't have _ to

live like a ref - u - gee (don't have to live like a ref - u - gee). _____

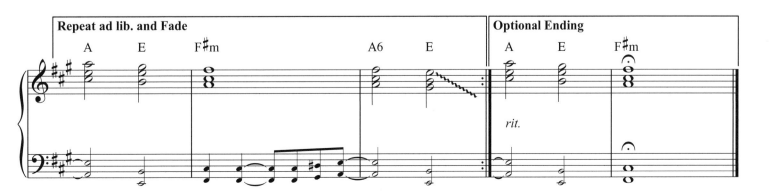

Repeat ad lib. and Fade

Optional Ending

rit.

Right Now

Words and Music by Edward Van Halen, Alex Van Halen, Michael Anthony and Sammy Hagar

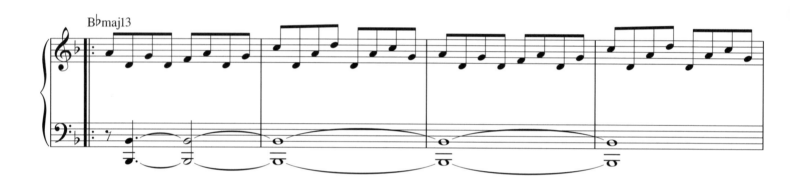

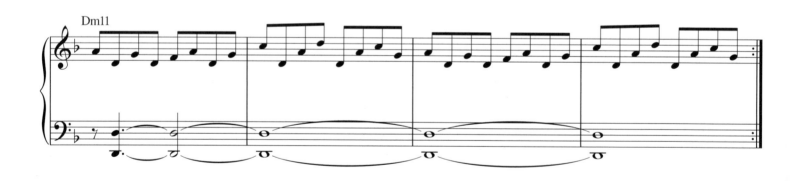

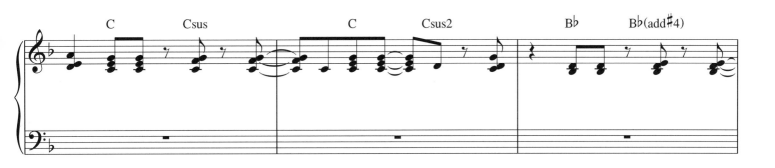

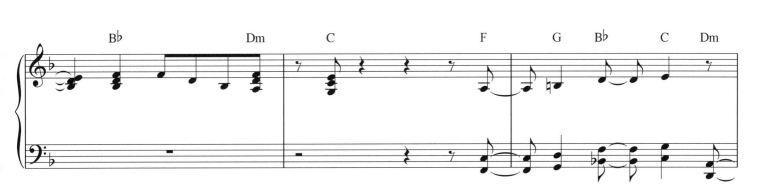

202

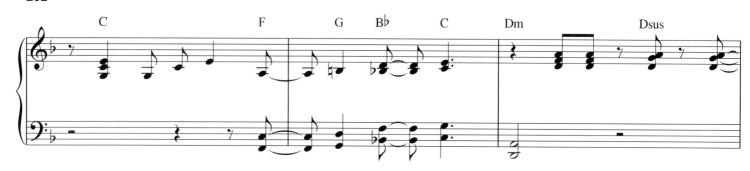
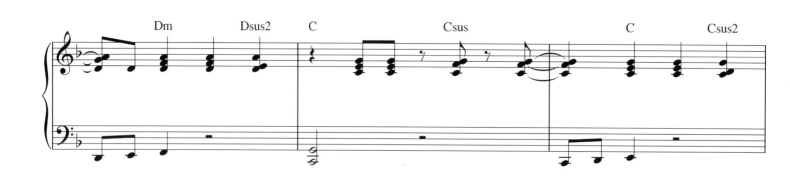

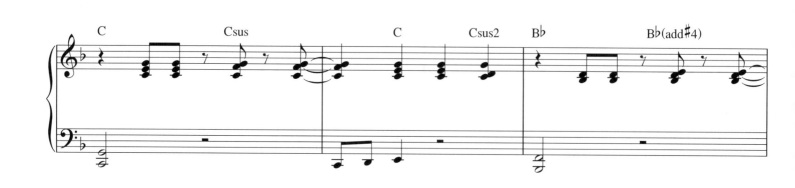

Don't wan - na wait 'til to - mor - row.
You miss a beat, you lose a rhy - thm,

Why put it off an - oth - er day.___
and noth-ing falls in - to place.___

One by one, lit - tle prob - lems ___
On - ly missed by a frac - tion, ___

now you got - ta run _____ to get e - ven.
just _____ trad - ing one _____ for the oth - er.

Play Fill 1 (2nd time)

Make fu - ture plans, ___ don't dream a - bout
Work - ing so hard ___ to make it ___

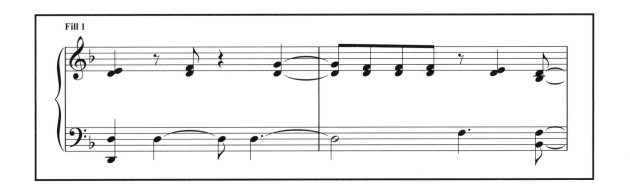

Fill 1

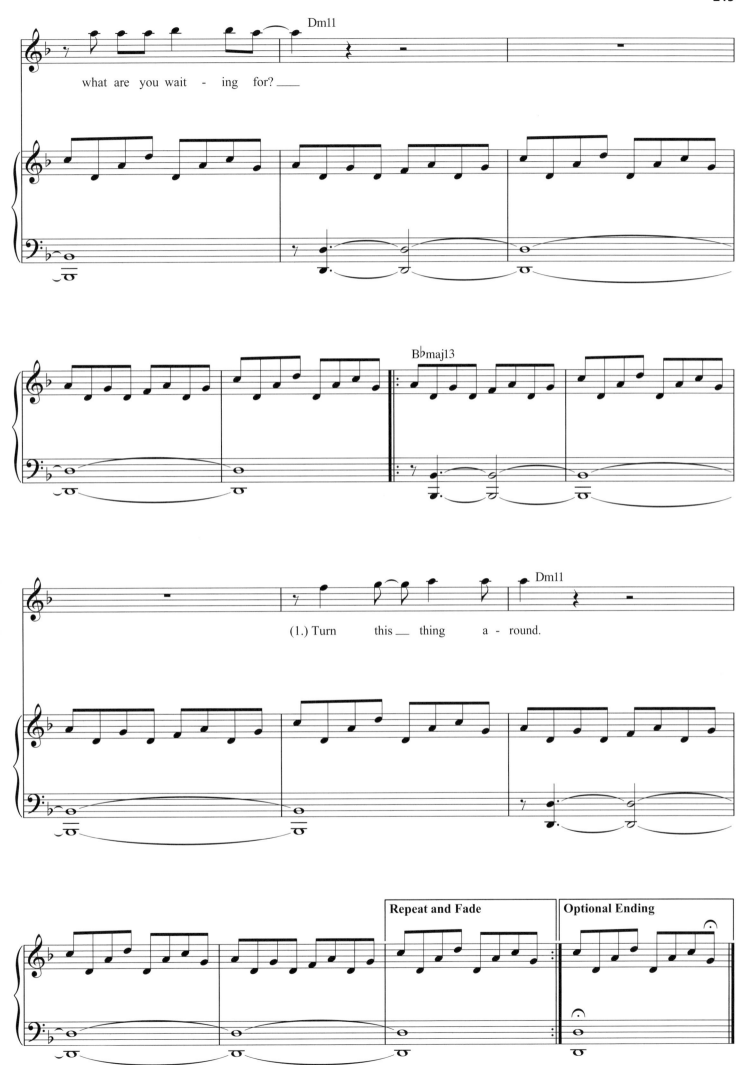

what are you wait - ing for? ___

(1.) Turn this ___ thing a - round.

Repeat and Fade　　　　**Optional Ending**

Right Place, Wrong Time

Words and Music by Mac Rebennack

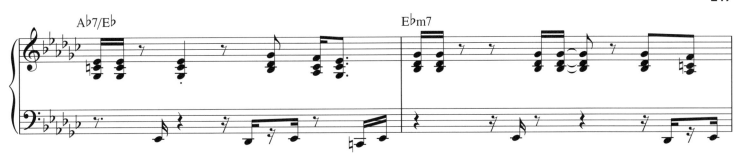

I been in the right place, _ but it must-'ve been the

wrong time. _ I'd 've said the right thing, ___ but I must-'ve used the

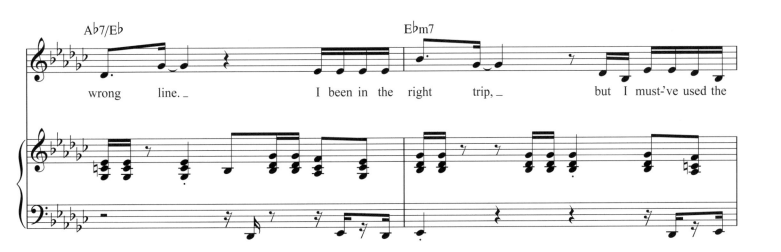

wrong line. _ I been in the right trip, _ but I must-'ve used the

* *Organ parts notated at pitch.*

in - se - cur - i - ty. __ But I been in the wrong place, _ but it must-'ve been the

right time. _ I been in the right place, but it must-'ve been the

wrong song. _   I been in the right vein,   but it seemed like the

wrong arm. _   'Cause I been in the right world,   but it seems like it's

wrong,   wrong,   wrong, —   wrong,   wrong. —

Vocal out

Organ out

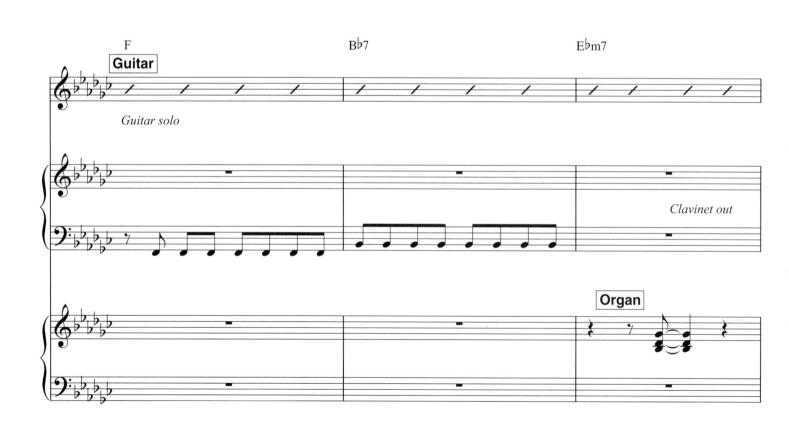

Guitar solo

Clavinet out

get on out - ta here? 'Cause I been in the right place, but it must-'ve been the

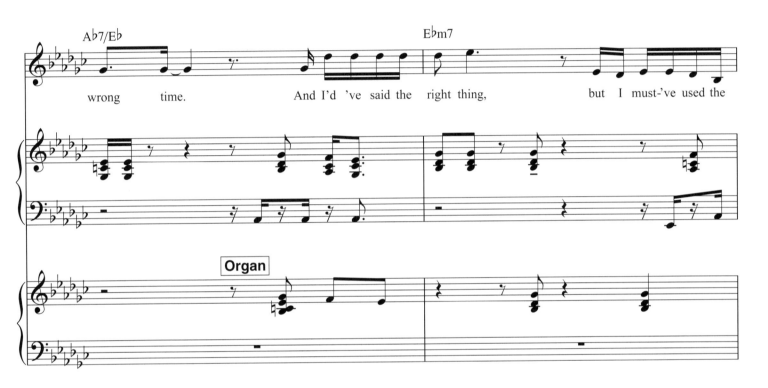

wrong time. And I'd 've said the right thing, but I must-'ve used the

Organ

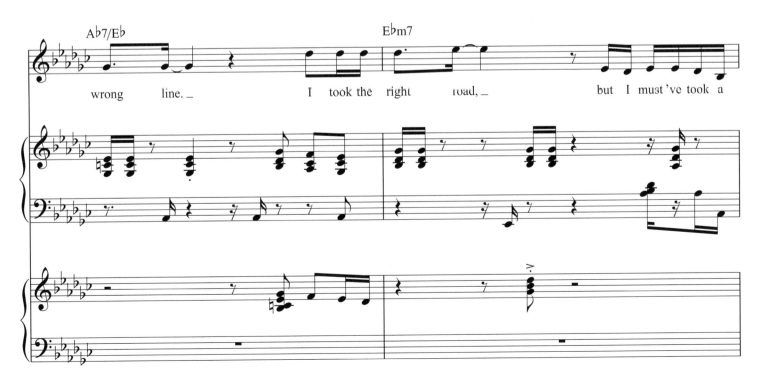

wrong line. _ I took the right road, _ but I must've took a

wrong turn. _ I took a right move, but I made it at the

wrong time. _ I been in the right trip, but I made it in the

wrong car. ___   Head was in a good place,   and   I'm won-d'ring what it's

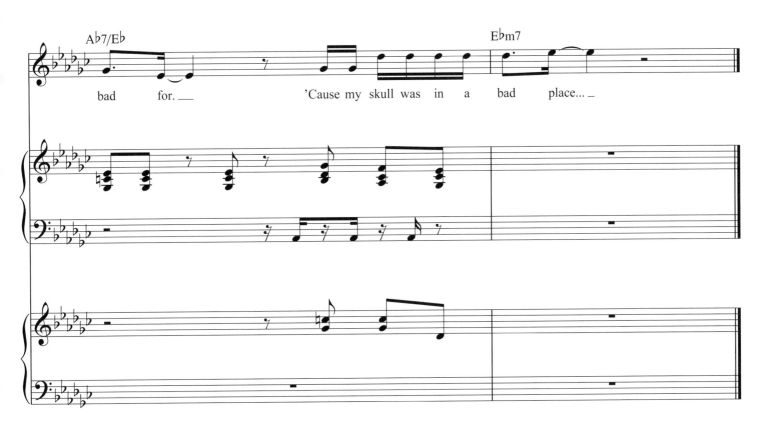

bad for. ___   'Cause my skull was in a bad place... ___

Roundabout

Words and Music by Jon Anderson and Steve Howe

*Keyboard 2 is an arrangement of guitar and bass parts.

Play L.H. both times

Using the 2⅔' organ drawbar doubles the line, an octave and a fifth above written pitch.

*Pattern is arpeggiated electronically. Played steadily, without regard for song tempo.

Moderately fast, as before (♩ = 126)

Arpeggiator continues uninterrupted

In and a - round the lake,

Mellotron

242

244

Runaway

Words and Music by Max Crook and Del Shannon

* *Originally recorded a half step lower and raised in production.*

And I ___ won - der (a) where she will stay, __

__ my lit - tle run-a - way, ___ (a)

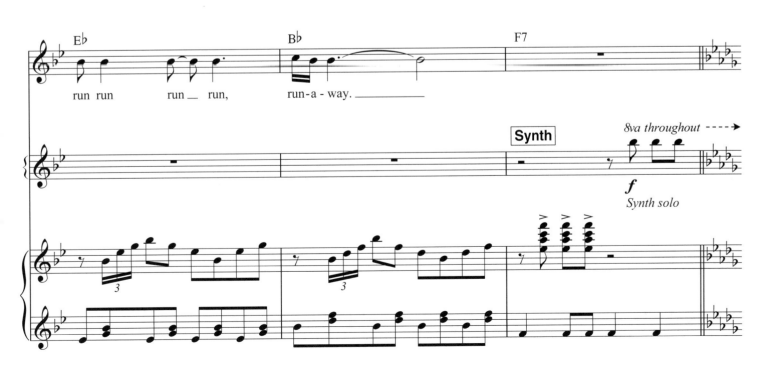

run run run __ run, run-a - way. ___

Synth

8va throughout - - - - →

f

Synth solo

I'm (a) walk - ing____ in the rain;____

Solo ends **mp**

tears are fall - ing, and I_____ feel the pain._____ (a) Wish-ing you were _

6th Avenue Heartache

Words and Music by Jakob Dylan

*Guitar staff conatins signature lines and solo as recorded.

drawn on me,_____ and now it's drawn me in:_____ well, Sixth Av - e - nue

heart - ache._____ And the same____ black line____ that was drawn on you____ was

drawn on me,_____ and now it's drawn me in:_____ well, Sixth Av - e - nue

yeah, _____ Sixth Av - e - nue heart - ache, heart -

ache.

(2., 3.,...) *Lead vocal tacet*

Dobro cues

Smokin'

Words and Music by Tom Scholz and Brad Delp

Keyboards is an arrangement of Guitar, Bass and Drums.

D.S. al Coda

Soul Sacrifice

By Carlos Santana

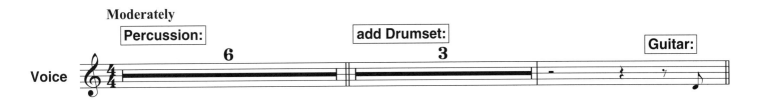

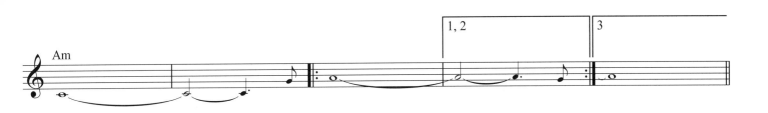

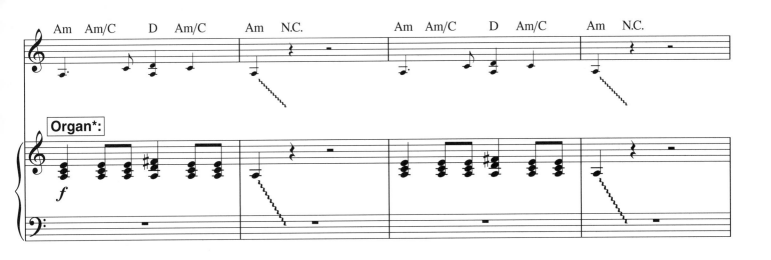

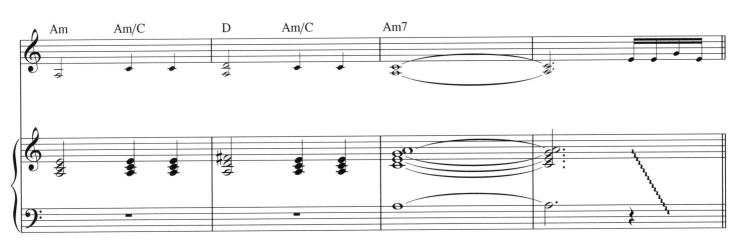

* *Organ part notated at pitch.*

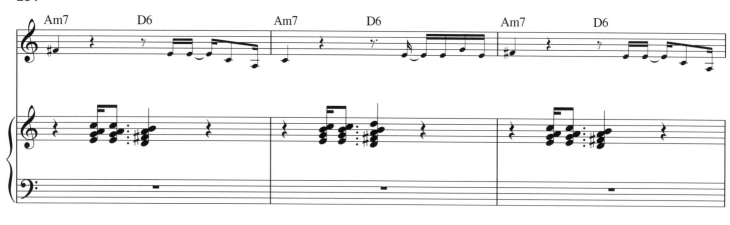

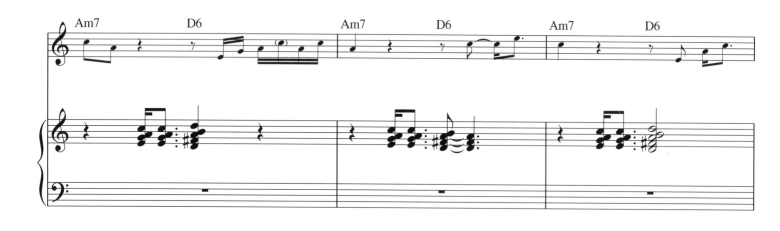

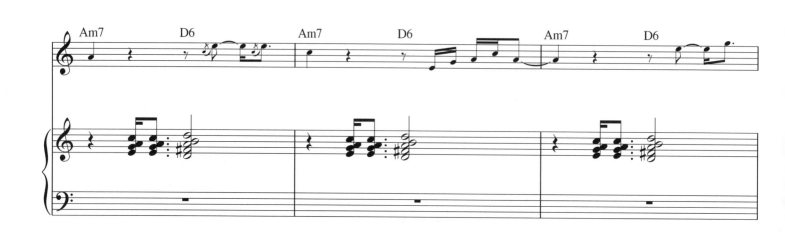

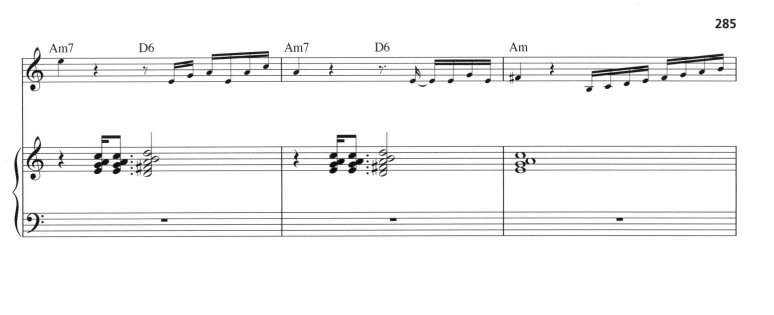

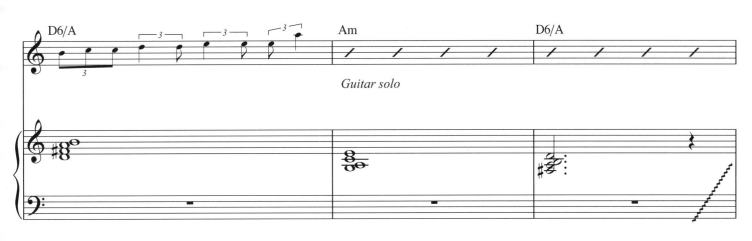

Guitar solo

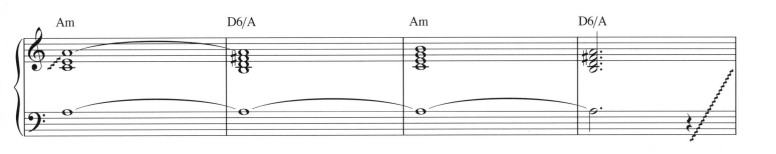

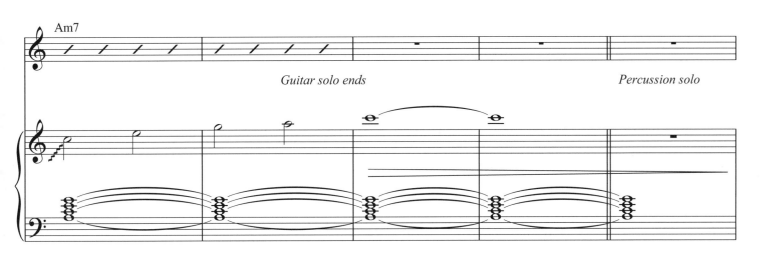

Guitar solo ends

Percussion solo

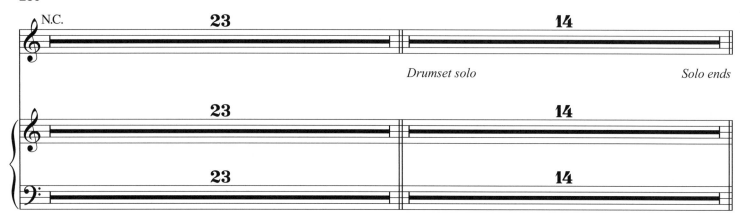

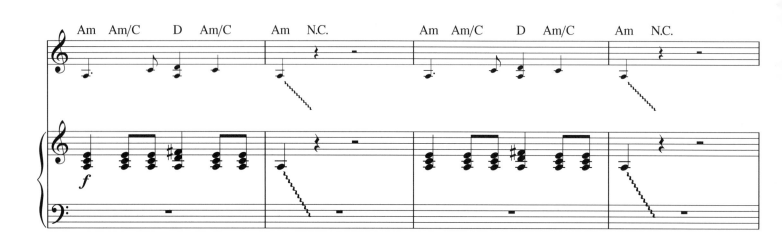

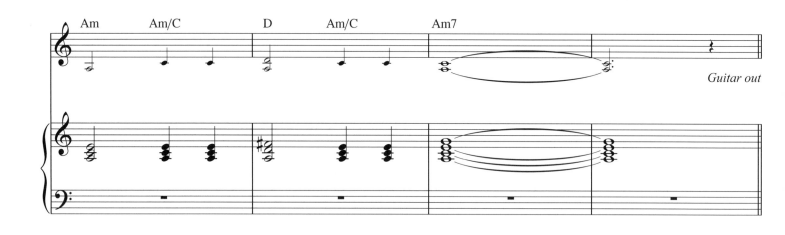

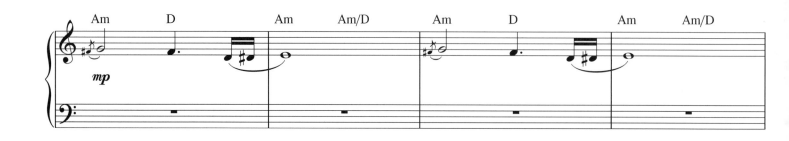

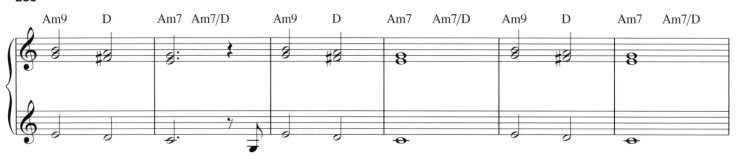

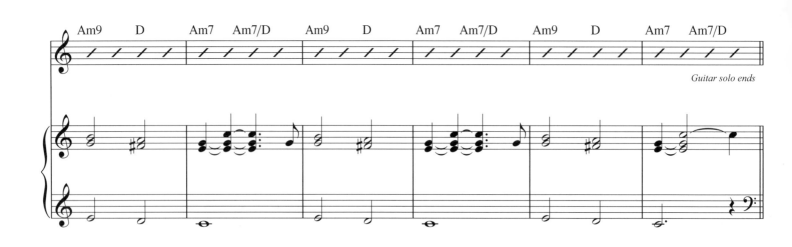

Guitar solo ends

Organ solo

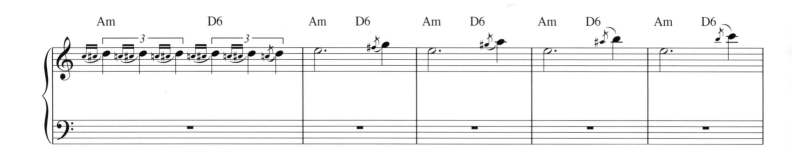

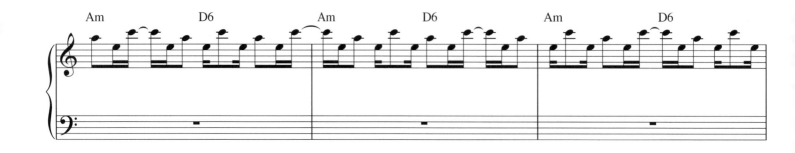

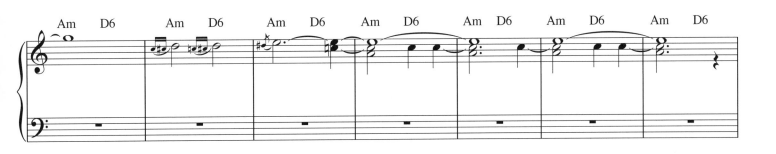

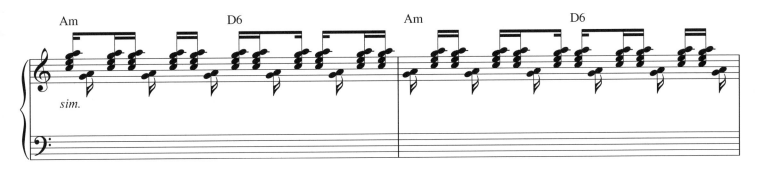

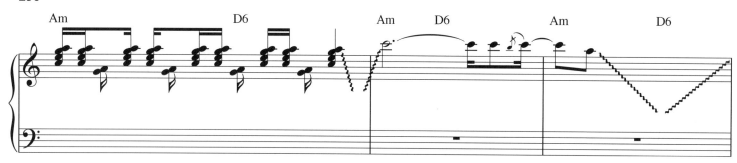

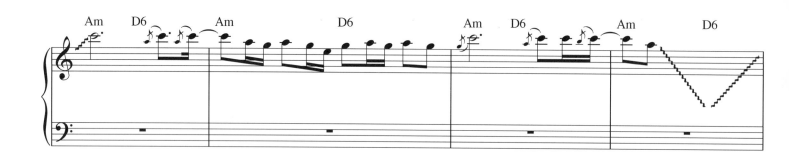

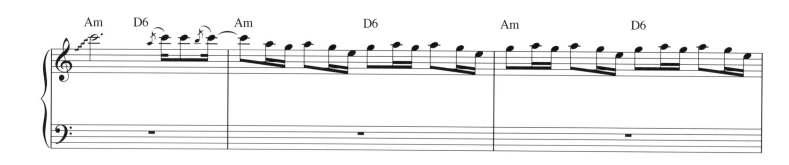

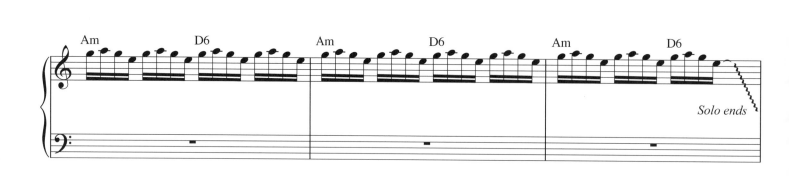

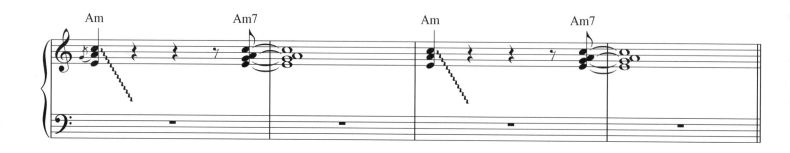

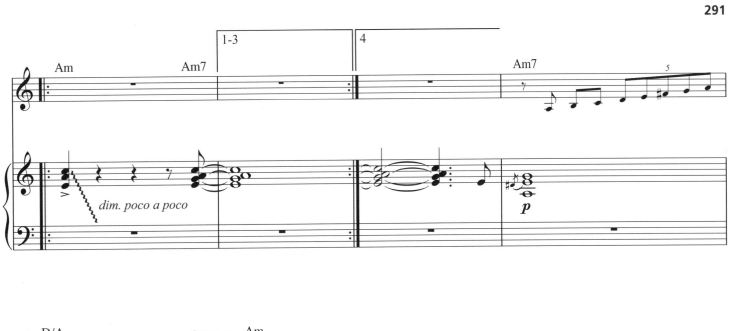

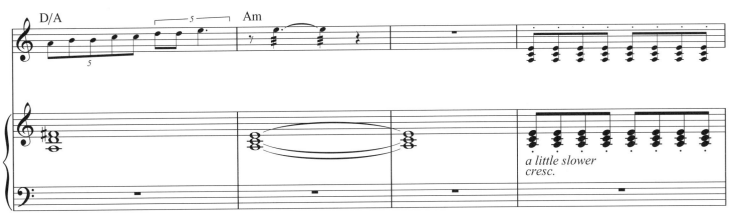

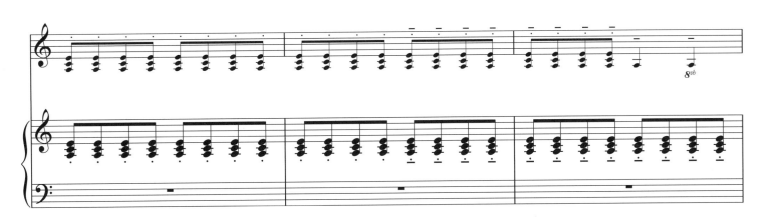

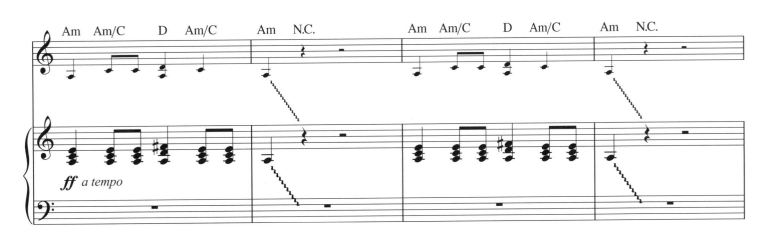

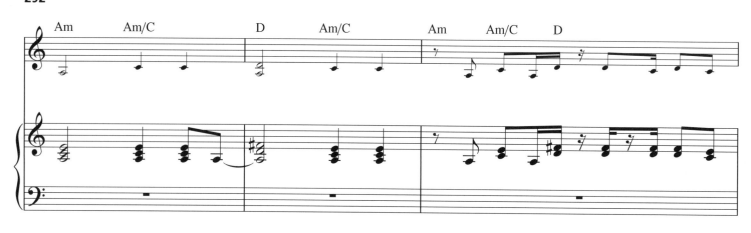

Takin' It to the Streets

Words and Music by Michael McDonald

(Tak - in' it to ___ the streets.)

Repeat ad lib. and Fade

(Tak - in' it to ___ the streets.)

(Tak - in' it to ___ the streets.)

Optional Ending

(Tak - in' it to ___ the streets.)

With a Little Help from My Friends

Words and Music by John Lennon and Paul McCartney

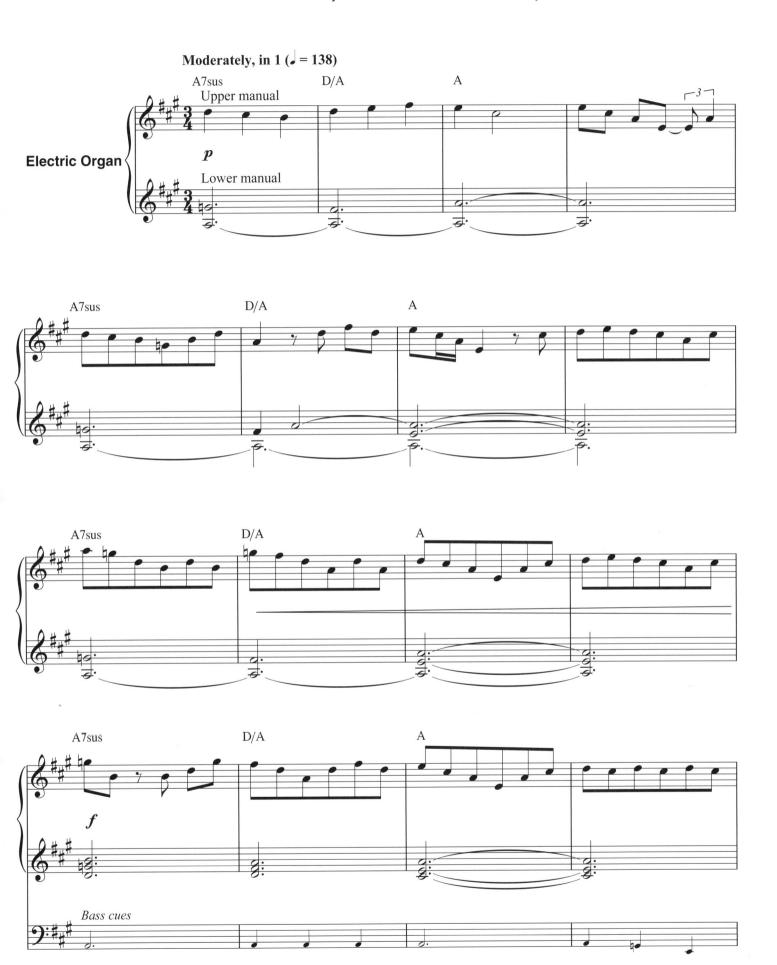

(Ooh, ooh, ooh.)

Repeat ad lib. and Fade

(Ooh, ooh, ooh.)

Optional Ending

(Ooh, ooh, ooh.)

rit.